N. F. PIMM

RAPID REVISION

MATHEMATICS

RAPID REVISION NOTES

MATHEMATICS

by

M. J. Powell

CELTIC REVISION AIDS

CELTIC REVISION AIDS
30–32 Gray's Inn Road,
London WC1X 8JL

© C.E.S.

First published 1980
Reprinted 1980, 1982, 1983

ISBN 0 86305 040 9

All rights reserved

Printed and bound in Great Britain by
Cox & Wyman Ltd, Reading

CONTENTS

INTRODUCTION AND FOREWORD	ix
FACTORS AND MULTIPLES	1
Notes and Examples	1
Practice Questions	2
FRACTIONS	3
Notes and Examples	3
Practice Questions	4
DECIMAL FRACTIONS	5
Notes and Examples	5
Practice Questions	6
RATIO	7
Notes and Examples	7
Practice Questions	7
PERCENTAGE	8
Notes and Examples	8
Practice Questions	9
SIMPLE AND COMPOUND INTEREST	10
Notes and Examples	10
Practice Questions	12
INDICES	12
Notes and Examples	12
Practice Questions	13
USE OF LOGARITHM TABLES	14
Notes and Examples	14
Practice Questions	16
USE OF TABLES OF SQUARES AND SQUARE ROOTS	16
Notes and Examples	16
Practice Questions	17

USE OF TABLE OF RECIPROCALS	17
Notes and Examples	17
Practice Questions	18
AVERAGES AND AVERAGE SPEED	18
Notes and Examples	18
Practice Questions	19
FACTORS AND THE REMAINDER THEOREM	20
Notes and Examples	20
Practice Questions	22
MENSURATION	24
Notes and Examples	24
Practice Questions	28
LINEAR EQUATIONS	31
Notes and Examples	31
Practice Questions	32
PROBLEMS INVOLVING LINEAR QUESTIONS	33
Notes and Examples	33
Practice Questions	35
QUADRATIC EQUATIONS	35
Notes and Examples	35
Practice Questions	38
PROBLEMS INVOLVING	
QUADRATIC EQUATIONS	38
Notes and Examples	38
Practice Questions	39
SIMULTANEOUS EQUATIONS	
(LINEAR EQUATIONS IN TWO UNKNOWNS)	40
Notes and Examples	40
Practice Questions	42

SIMULTANEOUS EQUATIONS (1 LINEAR, 1 QUADRATIC) — 42
- Notes and Examples — 42
- Practice Questions — 43

PROBLEMS INVOLVING SIMULTANEOUS EQUATIONS — 43
- Notes and Examples — 43
- Practice Questions — 44

GRAPHS — 45
- Notes and Examples — 45
- Practice Questions — 47

TRIGONOMETRY — 58
- Notes and Examples — 58
- Practice Questions — 62

VARIATION — 69
- Notes and Examples — 69
- Practice Questions — 71

PLANE GEOMETRY — 72
- Notes and Examples — 72
- Practice Questions — 86

EVERYDAY ARITHMETIC — 98
- Notes and Examples — 98
- Practice Questions — 101

QUICK TESTS A AND B — 103

FINAL TESTS 1 AND 2 — 108

ANSWERS TO NUMERICAL QUESTIONS — 115

EXAMINATION TECHNIQUE — 125

SERIES INTRODUCTION

Celtic Revision Aids Rapid Revision Notes are designed for use by students studying for CSE or 'O' level examinations.

The syllabus content has been divided into a number of fairly short and self-contained sections. For each section, the facts relating to that part of the syllabus are given as a series of easy-to-follow notes. Examples are given as appropriate and the section is concluded by giving a number of practice examination questions. Where these questions involve numerical work the correct answers are given at the end of the book.

The book is rounded off by a section on examination technique and you are strongly recommended to read these suggestions carefully.

These Rapid Revision Notes should be used to remind you of the essential facts of the subject as you prepare for the examination. Further practice in examination technique and familiarity with actual examination questions can be gained by using the Celtic Revision Aids Model Answers 'O' level and Multiple Choice 'O' level books for this subject.

AUTHOR'S FOREWORD

This book is designed to give the student a thorough revision course on the traditional mathematical contents of the 'O' level, C.S.E. and other 16+ examinations. The book is arranged in sections on the mathematical topics commonly found in these examinations.

Each section consists of short explanations of the important points of the topic which are then illustrated by a selection of worked examples. The student should study these carefully before attempting the questions which follow. The questions in each exercise are carefully graded, and include questions which are similar to the preceding worked examples. Thus the student is able to resolve quickly any difficulties which may occur and build up self-confidence in his mathematical ability.

Finally Quick Tests A and B consist of short, straight forward questions, while Tests 1 and 2 should, as far as possible, be worked under examination conditions.

The author has used his long, successful experience as a teacher and examiner in compiling the questions set in this book in order that the student gets practice at answering the types of questions set, and of working up to, and at, the standard required in order to achieve success in his examination.

M.J.P., 1979

FACTORS AND MULTIPLES

FACTORS

When two or more numbers are multiplied together they are said to be **factors** of the resulting product number.

E.g. $3 \times 4 \times 5 = 60$, therefore 3, 4, 5 are factors of 60.

A **prime number** is a number which is only divisible by itself and 1.
E.g. the first four prime numbers are 2, 3, 5, 7.

N.B. 1 is not a prime number.

A number which is a factor of two or more given numbers is called a **common factor** of the given numbers. The **H.C.F. (Highest Common Factor)** of the given numbers is the greatest of the common factors.

E.g. the factors of 24 are 1, 2, 3, 4, 6, 8, 12, 24.
    The factors of 36 are 1, 2, 3, 4, 6, 9, 12, 18, 36.
    The common factors of 24 and 36 are 1, 2, 3, 4, 6 and 12.
    The H.C.F. of 24 and 36 is 12.

MULTIPLES

A **multiple** of a given number is a number which is exactly divisible by the given number, i.e. a number having the given number as a factor.

E.g. 6, 9, 30 are multiples of 3.

A number which is a multiple of two or more given numbers is called a **common multiple** of the given numbers. The **L.C.M. (Lowest Common Multiple)** of the given numbers is the smallest of their common multiples.

E.g. the multiples of 6 are 6, 12, 18, 24, 30, 36, 42, 48, 54 . . . . . .
    The multiples of 8 are 8, 16, 24, 32, 40, 48, 56 . . . . . .
    Common multiples of 6 and 8 are 24, 48 . . . . . .
    The L.C.M. of 6 and 8 is 24.

The square root of a given number is the number whose square is the given number.

E.g. 4 is the square root of 16 since $4 \times 4 = 4^2 = 16$.

EXAMPLES

1. Express 24 and 42 as the product of prime numbers. Hence find their H.C.F. and L.C.M.

   ```
   2 | 24        2 | 42
   2 | 12        3 | 21
   2 |  6            7
         3
   ```

   $24 = \underline{2^3 \times 3}$ $42 = \underline{2 \times 3 \times 7}$

   H.C.F. of 24 and 42 = $2 \times 3 = \underline{6}$
   L.C.M. of 24 and 42 = $2^3 \times 3 \times 7 = \underline{168}$

2. Express 30625 in prime factors and hence find the square root of 30625.

   ```
   5 | 30625
   5 |  6125
   5 |  1225
   5 |   245
   7 |    49
             7
   ```

   $30625 = 5^4 \times 7^2$
   $\therefore \sqrt{30625} = 5^2 \times 7$
   $= \underline{175}$

PRACTICE QUESTIONS

1. (i) Express 156 as the product of prime factors.
   (ii) Find all the factors of 108.
   (iii) Express 36 and 126 in prime factors and find their H.C.F. and L.C.M.

2. Express 980100 in prime factors and hence find $\sqrt{980100}$.

3. The product of two numbers is $2^3 \times 3^2 \times 7^3 \times 11$. One of the numbers is 588. Find the other number.

4. What is the least number of bricks in a pile if when I count them 2 at a time, 6 at a time, or 14 at a time, there is always 1 odd brick left?

5. On one side of a road there are lamp standards 40m apart; on the other side there are telegraph poles 65m apart. At a certain place they are exactly opposite each other. When will they be exactly opposite each other next? How many telegraph poles are there between these two positions?

6. Express 63504 in prime factors and hence find the square root of 63504.

7. Express 216000 in prime factors and hence find its cube root.

8. Find the number of pieces, each 3·75cm long, which can be cut from a piece of thread 10m long. What length of thread is there left?

9. 50 lamp standards are to be erected at 75m intervals along the side of a straight road. What will be the distance between the first and last lamp standards?

On the opposite side of the road 36 poles are to be spaced equally so that the first and last poles coincide with the first and last lamp standards. What must be the space between consecutive posts?

FRACTIONS

A fraction of the form $\frac{a}{b}$ (where a and b are numbers) is unaltered in value if the **numerator (top)** and **denominator (bottom)** are both multiplied by, or both divided by the same number (not zero).

When simplifying expressions the order of working is (1) brackets; (2) of, $\times$, $\div$; (3) +, −.

EXAMPLES

1. Simplify (i) $\frac{2}{3} \times 2\frac{1}{4} + \frac{1}{5}$ (ii) $(2\frac{1}{7} \times 4\frac{2}{3}) - (2\frac{5}{6} + 1\frac{3}{8})$

   (i) $\frac{2}{3} \times 2\frac{1}{4} + \frac{1}{5}$

   $= \frac{2}{3} \times \frac{9}{4} + \frac{1}{5}$

   $= \frac{1\cancel{2}}{1\cancel{3}} \times \frac{\cancel{9}^3}{\cancel{4}_2} + \frac{1}{5}$

   $= \frac{3}{2} + \frac{1}{5}$

   $= \frac{15}{10} + \frac{2}{10}$

   $= \frac{17}{10} = \underline{1\frac{7}{10}}$

   (ii) $(2\frac{1}{7} \times 4\frac{2}{3}) - (2\frac{5}{6} + 1\frac{3}{8})$

   $= (\frac{\cancel{15}^5}{\cancel{7}_1} \times \frac{\cancel{14}^2}{\cancel{3}_1}) - (3 + \frac{5}{6} + \frac{3}{8})$

   $= 10 - (3 + \frac{20}{24} + \frac{9}{24})$

   $= 10 - (3\frac{29}{24})$

   $= 10 - 4\frac{5}{24}$

   $= \underline{5\frac{19}{24}}$

3

2. Simplify (i) $\dfrac{3(x + 2)}{4} - \dfrac{5x}{6}$ (ii) $\dfrac{15a^3b}{12x^2y^3} \div \dfrac{10ab^2}{9xy^6}$

(i) $\dfrac{3(x + 2)}{4} - \dfrac{5x}{6}$

$= \dfrac{9(x + 2)}{12} - \dfrac{10x}{12}$

$= \dfrac{9x + 18 - 10x}{12}$

$= \underline{\dfrac{18 - x}{12}}$

(ii) $\dfrac{15a^3b}{12x^2y^3} \div \dfrac{10ab^2}{9xy^6}$

$= \dfrac{\cancel{15}^3 \cancel{a^3}^{a^2} \cancel{b}}{\cancel{12}_4 \cancel{x^2}_x y^3} \times \dfrac{\cancel{9}^3 x \cancel{y^6}^{y^3}}{\cancel{10}_2 a \cancel{b^2}_b}$

$= \underline{\dfrac{9a^2y^3}{8xb}}$

PRACTICE QUESTIONS

1. Calculate (i) $3\tfrac{3}{8} + 4\tfrac{1}{3}$ (ii) $5\tfrac{1}{8} + 3\tfrac{2}{6}$
   (iii) $4\tfrac{2}{3} \div 1\tfrac{1}{10}$ (iv) $\tfrac{3}{4}$ of $7\tfrac{1}{3}$

2. Simplify (i) $\dfrac{3x}{4} + \dfrac{x}{2} - \dfrac{2x}{3}$ (ii) $\dfrac{2}{3a} + \dfrac{3}{ab} - \dfrac{1}{a}$

3. Simplify (i) $5\tfrac{1}{2} - 2\tfrac{1}{2}$ (ii) $\tfrac{1}{2}$ of $12\tfrac{1}{2}$
   (iii) $5\tfrac{5}{3} \times \tfrac{3}{5}$ (iv) $4\tfrac{3}{8} - 1\tfrac{5}{6} + \tfrac{7}{12}$

4. Simplify (i) $\tfrac{3}{4}$ of $2\tfrac{2}{3} - 1\tfrac{2}{6}$ (ii) $5\tfrac{1}{8} - 1\tfrac{2}{3} - 2\tfrac{7}{12}$

5. Simplify $(\tfrac{9}{16} \times 1\tfrac{2}{3}) + (\tfrac{9}{16} + 1\tfrac{2}{3})$

6. Evaluate (i) $(\frac{12}{35} \div \frac{3}{14}) \div 1\frac{1}{4}$ (ii) $\frac{6ab^2}{5p^3} \div \frac{4a^2b}{25p^4}$

7. Simplify (i) $\frac{1}{6} - \frac{3 - 7x}{3}$ (ii) $\frac{2}{5} - \frac{2(2 - x)}{10}$

8. Simplify (i) $\frac{14x^4y^3}{21x^8y^2}$ (ii) $\frac{4a^2b}{5xy^3} \times \frac{10xy^4}{6a^3b}$

9. A car travels at a steady speed of $27\frac{1}{2}$ km per hour. How far will it travel in (i) $\frac{1}{4}$ hour, (ii) $1\frac{1}{2}$ hours, (iii) x mins?

10. Simplify (i) $\frac{3(x + 1)}{x - 2} + \frac{4x}{5}$

    (ii) $\frac{3x + 4}{4x} - \frac{(2 - x)}{2x} + 2$

11. (i) Express as a fraction in its lowest terms $\frac{4\frac{3}{4} - 3\frac{7}{18}}{7\frac{1}{3} - 1\frac{1}{2}}$

    (ii) Simplify $\frac{4x + 8}{x^2 - 2x - 3} \times \frac{x^2 + 3x + 2}{6x^2 + 24x + 24}$

DECIMAL FRACTIONS

The decimal point always separates the whole numbers from the fractional parts. Reason carefully where the decimal point should be placed in an answer. Estimate the result first.

EXAMPLES

1. Evaluate $13 \cdot 64 \times 2 \cdot 73$
   (Estimated answer: $13 \times 3 = 39$)

$$\begin{array}{r} 1364 \times 273 \\ \underline{273} \\ 272800 \\ 95480 \\ \underline{4092} \\ 372372 \end{array}$$

hence $13 \cdot 64 \times 2 \cdot 73 = \underline{37 \cdot 2372}$

2. Evaluate $78 \cdot 8942 \div 1 \cdot 54$
   (Estimated answer: $80 \div 2 = 40$)

   $$\frac{78 \cdot 8942}{1 \cdot 54} = \frac{7889 \cdot 42}{154 \cdot 00}$$

   ```
              51·23
       154 )7889·42
            770
            189
            154
            354
            308
            462
            462
            ...
   ```

   hence $78 \cdot 8942 \div 1 \cdot 54 = \underline{51 \cdot 23}$

PRACTICE QUESTIONS

NO TABLES OR CALCULATORS TO BE USED IN THIS EXERCISE

1. Add $3 \cdot 45$, $12 \cdot 6$, $7 \cdot 83$ and $18 \cdot 459$.

2. Subtract $35 \cdot 89$ from $120 \cdot 25$.

3. Multiply $6 \cdot 57$ by $8 \cdot 34$.

4. Divide $19 \cdot 8105$ by $8 \cdot 43$.

5. Evaluate $266 \cdot 29 \div 0 \cdot 47$ correct to 3 sig. figs.

6. Calculate $3 \cdot 54 \times 7 \cdot 28$ and give the product correct to one decimal place.

7. Write in standard form

   (i) $\dfrac{99 \times 10^{-1}}{(3 \times 10^3)^2}$

   (ii) $\dfrac{377 \cdot 86}{0 \cdot 007}$

8. Multiply $0 \cdot 0479$ by $236 \cdot 58$ and write the result in standard form.

RATIO

Ratio is another form of fraction. Increase £60 in the ratio 4:3 means multiply £60 by $\frac{4}{3}$. The result is £80, and the ratio new:old = 80:60 = 4:3.

Divide £42 in the ratio 4:3 means that first £42 has to be divided into 7 (i.e. 4 + 3) equal parts, and rearranged into two portions $\frac{4}{7}$ and $\frac{3}{7}$, i.e. £24 and £18.

EXAMPLE

A coach company carried 15,000 passengers last year at an average fare of £3 each. This year the company expects the number of passengers to decrease in the ratio of 3:5 in comparison with last year. By how much must the average fare per passenger be increased if the company is not to suffer a loss of revenue?

No. of passengers to be carried this year = $15,000 \times \frac{3}{5}$ = 9,000.

Last year's revenue = £3 × 15,000 = £45,000.

This year's average fare $\geqslant \dfrac{£45,000}{9,000}$ = £5.

<u>Increase in average fare must be at least £2.</u>

PRACTICE QUESTIONS

1. (i) Increase 72 in the ratio 9:4.
   (ii) In what ratio must 240 be decreased to become 160?
   (iii) A legacy of £6,500 is divided between two persons in the ratio 6:7. What amount does each receive?

2. A bus company carried 100,000 passengers last month at an average fare of 75p each. This month the company expects the number of passengers to decrease in the ratio of 4:5, and the average fare to increase in the ratio of 6:5 over last month's fare. What will be the decrease in revenue for this month?

3. A map is drawn to scale 5cm represents 8km.
   (a) Express this scale in the form 1:n.
   (b) Calculate the actual distance, in kilometres, between two towers that are 7·4cm apart on the map.
   (c) Calculate the map length of a road which is actually 10km 720m long.
   (d) Calculate the area, in square kilometres, of a lake whose area on the map is 3·5cm^2.

4. The number of bacteria in a culture increases in the ratio 5:3 every hour. If there were 27,000 at a certain time,
   (a) how many were there an hour previously, and
   (b) how many will there be 3 hours later?

5. ABC is a triangle. D is a point in AB through which a line DE is drawn parallel to BC, cutting AC at E. Through E, a line EF is drawn parallel to AB cutting BC at F. If BF = 10cm, FC = 12cm, EC = 9cm and EF = 8·1cm, find the lengths of AE and AD.

6. (i) If $3x + 4y = x + 16y$ find the ratio x:y.
   (ii) Find the ratio of p:q if
   (a) p exceeds q by 35% of q.
   (b) p exceeds q by x% of p.

7. A sum of money is made up of equal numbers of 50 pence pieces, 10 pence pieces and 5 pence pieces. The total value of the coins is £455. How many of each type of coin is there?

PERCENTAGE

Percentage is another form of fraction, i.e. $17\% = \dfrac{17}{100}$.

Increase £30 by 15% means multiply £30 by $\dfrac{115}{100}$.

N.B. Profit percentage is based on the cost price unless stated otherwise in the question.

EXAMPLE

A dealer bought two cars for £1,750 each. If he makes a profit of 36% on selling the first car calculate his selling price. He sells the second car for £2,200. Calculate his percentage profit on the second car, correct to the nearest percent.

$$\text{Profit on first car} = 36\% \text{ of } £1,750$$
$$= \dfrac{36}{100} \times 1,750$$
$$= £36 \times 17\cdot5 = £630$$
$$\text{Selling price} = \underline{£2,380}$$

$$\text{Profit on second car} = £2,200 - £1,750 = £450.$$

$$\text{Percentage profit} = \frac{450}{1750} \times 100\%$$

$$= 25 \cdot 7\%$$

$$= \underline{26\% \text{ to nearest percent}}$$

PRACTICE QUESTIONS

1. Express the following as percentages: $\frac{2}{3}$, $0 \cdot 73$, $2\frac{1}{8}$, $4:5$, $0 \cdot 368$.

2. Express the following as fractions in their lowest terms: 45%, $62\frac{1}{2}\%$, $7\frac{1}{2}\%$.

3. Find the value of (i) 60% of £3.75, (ii) $166\frac{2}{3}\%$ of £7.50.

4. (i) Increase £70 by 12%, (ii) Decrease 40 hours by 3%.

5. An article costing £5.60 is sold at a profit of 30%. What was the selling price?

6. A car is sold for £2,232 at a gain of 24%. What was the cost price of the car and how much profit was made?

7. A new car cost £3,750. It lost 25% of its value by the end of its first year. At the end of the next year it has lost 20% of its value at the beginning of that year. At the end of the next two years, it had lost 16% of its value at the beginning of the year per year. Calculate, to the nearest £, its value at the end of the fourth year.

8. A car which depreciated as the car in Q.7 above was worth £1,680 at the end of its fourth year. Calculate its cost when new, correct to the nearest £.

9. The marked price of an article in a shop is the price which will give the shopkeeper a profit of 25% on his cost price. He sells an article marked at £6.60, but gives a discount of 5p in £ to the customer. Whas was the shopkeeper's actual percentage profit on this article?

10. An examination consisted of three papers and the total possible mark on each paper was 200, 150 and 80 respectively. A student gained $87\frac{1}{2}\%$ of the possible marks on the first paper, 78% of the possible marks on the second paper and 65% of the possible marks on the last paper. Find the overall percentage marks of this student in the examination.

11. When petrol was 90p per gallon I used 40 gallons monthly. A price increase of 5% in the cost of petrol was announced and I immediately resolved to cut my consumption by 5%. How much money per month did I save?

12. A dealer bought two pianos for £580 each. What is the selling price if he sells the first piano at a profit of 35%? He then sells the second piano for £667. What was his percentage profit on the whole deal?

13. A haulage company finds that the cost of a particular journey is £208, and that 15% of this was the cost of fuel used, and 60% was for wages. Fuel price is increased from 90p to 99p per gallon, and wages are increased by 5%. What will be the new cost of this journey if the other charges remain constant? What is the percentage increase in the cost of this journey?

SIMPLE AND COMPOUND INTEREST

SIMPLE INTEREST

The **Simple Interest**, £I, on a Principal, £P for T years at R% per annum is given by:

$$I = \frac{PRT}{100}$$

The unit in which each quantity is measured is important. I will be in £ when P is in £, R in % per annum and T in years.

The total amount £A accrued on a Principal £P after T years at R% per annum simple interest is given by

$$A = P + \frac{PRT}{100}$$

i.e. $A = P\left(1 + \frac{RT}{100}\right)$

COMPOUND INTEREST

Compound Interest is the interest over a period calculated on the sum of the original principal plus the interest accrued over the previous period. If Compound Interest is reckoned at r% per annum, compounded annually, on an original principal of £P, the amount accrued £A at the end of n years is given by

$$A = P\left(1 + \frac{r}{100}\right)^n$$

Again the quantities must be measured in the units stated.

EXAMPLES

1. Find the simple interest on £664 after 9 months at 5% per annum. Find also the principal which will amount to £664 after 9 months at 5% per annum simple interest.

   £P = £664   T years = $\frac{3}{4}$ year   R% p.a. = 5% p.a.

   $$I = \frac{PRT}{100}$$

   $$= \frac{664 \times 5 \times 3}{100 \times 4}$$

   $$= \frac{249}{10}$$

   Simple interest is £24.90

   $$A = P + \frac{PRT}{100}$$

   $$A = P\left(1 + \frac{RT}{100}\right)$$

   $$664 = P\left(1 + \frac{5 \times 3}{100 \times 4}\right)$$

   $$= \frac{415}{400}P$$

   $$P = \frac{664 \times 400}{415}$$

   $$= 640$$

   The principal required is £640

2. Calculate the compound interest, correct to the nearest penny, on £725 at $12\frac{1}{2}$ per annum for $2\frac{1}{2}$ years.

	£	Interest
P at start of 1st year	725.00	1% — £7.25
I at 12%	87.00	
I at $\frac{1}{2}$%	3.625	

11

	£	Interest
P at start of 2nd year	815.625	1% — £8.1562
I at 12%	97.8744	
I at ½%	4.0781	
P at start of 3rd year	917.5775	1% — £9.1757
I at 6%	55.0542	
I at ¼%	2.2939	
Amount at end of 2½ years	974.9256	
Original P	725.	
Compound interest	249.9256	
Compound interest =	£249.93 to nearest p	

N.B. Work up to the fourth decimal place in order to obtain an answer correct to the nearest penny.

PRACTICE QUESTIONS

1. Find the simple interest on £1,530 for 2½ years at 5⅓% p.a.

2. Find the sum of money which will yield £480 simple interest in 2½ years at 6% p.a.

3. Find the principal which amounts to £350 after 2 years 8 months at 12½% p.a. simple interest.

4. Calculate the compound interest on £500 at 9% per annum for 2½ years.

5. A man invests £5,000 at 9% compound interest, compound yearly, Income tax at 33⅓% is deducted from each amount of annual interest. What is the net amount of the investment at the commencement of the third year?

6. A man borrows £1,000. Interest at the rate of 10% p.a. is added to the amount outstanding at the commencement of a year. He repays the debt in two equal instalments, one at the end of the first year and the other at the end of the second yer. What was the value of each instalment, correct to the nearest penny?

INDICES

If N is any number, other than zero, and p and q are any numbers, then:
- (i) $N^p \times N^q = N^{p+q}$
- (ii) $N^p \div N^q = N^{p-q}$

(iii) $(N^p)^q = N^{pq}$
(iv) $N^0 = 1$
(v) $N^{-p} = \dfrac{1}{N^p}$
(vi) $N^{\frac{p}{q}} = \sqrt[q]{N^p} = (\sqrt[q]{N})^p$

EXAMPLES

1. Find the exact value of (a) $3^{\frac{1}{3}} \times 3^{-\frac{4}{3}}$ (b) $9^{\frac{1}{4}} \div 9^{\frac{3}{4}}$ (c) $(2\frac{1}{4})^{\frac{3}{2}}$

   (a) $3^{\frac{1}{3}} \times 3^{-\frac{4}{3}} = 3^{(\frac{1}{3}-\frac{4}{3})} = 3^{-1} = \frac{1}{3}$

   (b) $9^{\frac{1}{4}} \div 9^{\frac{3}{4}} = 9^{(\frac{1}{4}-\frac{3}{4})} = 9^{-\frac{1}{2}} = \dfrac{1}{9^{\frac{1}{2}}} = \dfrac{1}{\sqrt{9}} = \frac{1}{3}$

   (c) $(2\frac{1}{4})^{\frac{3}{2}} = (\frac{9}{4})^{\frac{3}{2}} = (\sqrt{\frac{9}{4}})^3 = (\frac{3}{2})^3 = \frac{27}{8} = 3\frac{3}{8}$

2. Simplify $\left(\dfrac{3}{2x}\right)^{-2} + \left(\dfrac{16x^8}{81}\right)^{\frac{1}{4}}$

   $\left(\dfrac{3}{2x}\right)^{-2} = \left(\dfrac{2x}{3}\right)^2 = \dfrac{4x^2}{9} \cdot \left(\dfrac{16x^8}{81}\right)^{\frac{1}{4}} = \dfrac{2x^2}{3}$

   $\therefore \left(\dfrac{3}{2x}\right)^{-2} + \left(\dfrac{16x^8}{81}\right)^{\frac{1}{4}} = \dfrac{4x^2}{9} + \dfrac{2x^2}{3} = \dfrac{4x^2 + 6x^2}{9} = \underline{\dfrac{10x^2}{9}}$

PRACTICE QUESTIONS

1. Write down the exact values of 2^3, $16^{\frac{1}{2}}$, 5^{-3}, $4^{\frac{3}{2}}$, 121^{-1}

2. Simplify (i) $a^3 \times a^7$ (ii) $a^{\frac{3}{2}} \times a^{\frac{1}{2}}$
   (iii) $x^{-3} \times x^5$ (iv) $x^{16} \div x^8$
   (v) $b^3 \div b^{-2}$ (vi) $(c^3)^4$

3. Write down the exact values of 2^{-3}, $(\frac{1}{3})^{-2}$, 7^0, $32^{\frac{2}{5}}$, $125^{\frac{1}{3}}$, $100^{1.5}$, $27^{-\frac{1}{3}}$, $(\frac{1}{8})^{-\frac{2}{3}}$.

4. Simplify (i) $\left(\dfrac{1}{3a^2}\right)^{-1} + (625a^4)^{\frac{1}{2}}$

   (ii) $(-216x^6)^{\frac{1}{3}} + \left(\dfrac{1}{8x^6}\right)^{-\frac{1}{3}}$

5. Simplify (i) $(a^{-\frac{1}{3}} \div a^{\frac{2}{3}})^{-1}$ (ii) $(b^{\frac{2}{3}})^6$
   (iii) $(x^{\frac{2}{3}} \times x^{\frac{1}{2}})^6$ (iv) $1 \div (9y^4)^{-\frac{1}{2}}$

USE OF LOGARITHM TABLES

DEFINITION OF A LOGARITHM

If a number n can be expressed in the form a^x, the index x is called the logarithm of the number n, to the base a.

The base used in calculations is 10. $100 = 10^2$, so the logarithm of 100 (to the base 10) is 2. $1000 = 10^3$, so the logarithm of 1000 (to the base 10) is 3. Since 365 lies between 100 and 1000 the logarithm of 365 (to the base 10) lies between 2 and 3. The decimal part of the logarithm is obtained from the table of logarithms, and is ·5623. Thus the logarithm of 365 (to the base 10) is 2·5623.

Again, using base 10,
$0·1 = 10^{-1}$, so the logarithm of $0·1$ is -1, written $\bar{1}$,
and $0·01 = 10^{-2}$, so the logarithm of $0·01$ is -2, written $\bar{2}$.

Since $0·0243$ lies between $0·01$ and $0·1$ the logarithm of $0·0243$ lies between $\bar{2}$ and $\bar{1}$. The decimal part is again obtained from the table of logarithms and will always be positive. From the tables, row "24" column "3" we obtain ·3856. Thus the logarithm of $0·0243$ is $\bar{2}·3856$. Since logarithms are indices, laws of indices apply giving,

(i)   The logarithm of a product of two numbers P and Q is the sum of the logarithms of P and Q.

      i.e. $\log(P \times Q) = \log P + \log Q$.

(ii) The logarithm of the quotient of two number $\frac{P}{Q}$ is the logarithm of P minus the logarithm of Q.

      i.e. $\log\left(\frac{P}{Q}\right) = \log P - \log Q$.

(iii) The log of P^m is m times log P.

      i.e. $\log(P^m) = m \log P$.

EXAMPLES

Use logarithms to evaluate correct to 3 sig. figs.

(i) $593·4 \times 0·3596$ (ii) $\dfrac{(0·0234)^2}{8·052}$

(iii) $$\sqrt[4]{\left(\frac{0\cdot 3515 \times 42\cdot 74}{(6\cdot 21)^3}\right)}$$

(i)

number	log
593·4	2·7734
0·3596	$\bar{1}$·5558
	2·3292
antilog =	2134
product =	213·4 to 3 s.f.

(ii)

number	log
0·0234	$\bar{2}$·3692
	2
( )²	$\bar{4}$·7384
8·052	0·9059
	$\bar{5}$·8325
antilog =	6800
result =	0·00006800
	= 0·0000680 or $6\cdot 80 \times 10^{-5}$, to 3 s.f.

(iii) $$\sqrt[4]{\frac{N}{D}} = \sqrt[4]{\left(\frac{0\cdot 3515 \times 42\cdot 74}{(6\cdot 21)^3}\right)}$$

Numerator N	log	Denominator D	log
0·3515	$\bar{1}$·5459	6·21	0·7931
42·74	1·6308		3
N	1·1767	D	2·3793

Number	log
N	1·1767
D	2·3793
$\frac{N}{D}$	$\bar{2}$·7974
	$4\,\overline{|\bar{4}+2\cdot 7974}$
$\sqrt[4]{\frac{N}{D}}$	$\bar{1}$·6993

antilog = 5003
result = 0·5003 = <u>0·500 to 3 s.f.</u>

PRACTICE QUESTIONS

1. Using logarithms, evaluate the following, correct to three significant figures.
   (i) $36 \cdot 49 \times 725 \cdot 4$
   (ii) $0 \cdot 00415 \times 76 \cdot 52$
   (iii) $765 \cdot 3 \div 86 \cdot 9$
   (iv) $28 \cdot 42 \div 0 \cdot 004217$
   (v) $6 \cdot 24 \times 52 \cdot 15 \div 284 \cdot 7$
   (vi) $(72 \cdot 43)^5$
   (vii) $\sqrt[3]{834 \cdot 7}$
   (viii) $\sqrt[3]{0 \cdot 1256}$

2. Use logarithms to calculate the value of the following, correct to three significant figures

   (i) $\dfrac{76 \cdot 03 \times 872 \cdot 1}{674 \cdot 2 \times 0 \cdot 9971}$

   (ii) $\dfrac{(362 \cdot 1)^3}{78 \cdot 4 \times 965 \cdot 3}$

   (iii) $\sqrt{\dfrac{2 \cdot 015 \times 0 \cdot 123}{3 \cdot 28 \times 1 \cdot 19}}$

   (iv) $\sqrt[4]{\dfrac{6 \cdot 4 \times 11 \cdot 17}{(13 \cdot 8)^2}}$

USE OF TABLES OF SQUARES AND SQUARE ROOTS

Always estimate the answer before using these tables.

Find the square of $354 \cdot 2$ from the table of squares.
First estimate $300^2 = 90000$ and $400^2 = 160000$ so the square of $354 \cdot 2$ lies between 90,000 and 160,000. From the table we obtain 1254 as the first 4 significant figures in our result, thus $(354 \cdot 2)^2 = 125,400$ to 4 s.f.

Find the square root of 7875. First mark off the given number in periods of 2 digits starting at the decimal point. Look at the furthest left hand period. The greatest integer whose square is not more than 78 is 8. 8 is the first digit of the square root and each period corresponds to 1 digit in the square root. Check $80^2 = 6400$ and $90^2 = 8100$; so the square root required lies between 80 and 90. From the square root table we obtain 8874 thus $\sqrt{7875} = 88 \cdot 74 = 88 \cdot 7$ to 3 s.f.

EXAMPLE

Find, correct to 3 s.f. the square and the square root of the following numbers, (i) 165, (ii) $0 \cdot 753$

(i) $(165)^2$ Estimate $100^2 = 10,000$
                                            $200^2 = 40,000$

From table: 2723
∴ $(165)^2$ = 27,230
= <u>27,200 to 3 s.f.</u>

$\sqrt{165}$ · Estimate $10^2 = 100$
From table: 1285 $20^2 = 400$
∴ $\sqrt{165}$ = 12·85
= <u>12·9 to 3 s.f.</u>

(ii) $(0·753)^2$ Estimate $(0·7)^2 = 0·49$
  $(0·8)^2 = 0·64$

From table: 5670
∴ $(0·753)^2$ = 0·5670
= <u>0·567 to 3 s.f.</u>

$\sqrt{0·753}$ Estimate $0·8^2 = 0·64$
  $0·9^2 = 0·91$

From table: 8678
∴ $\sqrt{0·753}$ = 0·8678
= <u>0·868 to 3 s.f.</u>

PRACTICE QUESTIONS

1. Use the table of squares to evaluate, correct to 3 s.f. the square of,
   (i) 64·2, (ii) 0·345, (iii) 786·4, (iv) 0·09715.

2. Use the square root table to find, correct to 3 s.f. the square roots of,
   (i) 88·3, (ii) 0·451, (iii) 654·1,
   (iv) 7892, (v) 0·0047, (vi) 0·000678.

3. Evaluate, (i) $\sqrt{4·54}$ (ii) $(1·247)^2$
   (iii) $\dfrac{1}{\sqrt{2}}$ (iv) $\dfrac{3}{\sqrt{3}} + (\sqrt{3})^3$

   Give the answers correct to 2 decimal places.

USE OF TABLE OF RECIPROCALS

The reciprocal of 2 is $\frac{1}{2}$ i.e. 0·5

The reciprocal of 20 is $\frac{1}{20}$ i.e. 0·05

The reciprocal of 200 is $\frac{1}{200}$ i.e. 0·005

Thus the larger the number the smaller will be its reciprocal.

To find the reciprocal of 42·5 first estimate the result, $\frac{1}{40} = 0·025$

From the reciprocal table obtain 2353

thus $\dfrac{1}{42·5} = 0·02353$.

EXAMPLE

Find the reciprocals of (i) 187·4, (ii) 0·0354.

(i) $\dfrac{1}{187·4}$ Estimate $\frac{1}{100} = 0·01$

$\frac{1}{200} = 0·005$.

From table: 5336

∴ $\dfrac{1}{187·4} = \underline{0·005336 \text{ to 4 s.f.}}$

(ii) $\dfrac{1}{0·0354}$ Estimate $\dfrac{1}{0·03} = \dfrac{100}{3} = 33·3$

From table: 2825

∴ $\dfrac{1}{0·0354} = 28·25$ to 4 s.f.

PRACTICE QUESTIONS

Find the reciprocals of the following, giving the answers correct to 3 s.f.

- (i) 7·24
- (ii) 0·04521
- (iii) 287·3
- (iv) 0·5485
- (v) 168·2
- (vi) 0·007835
- (vii) 543800
- (viii) 201·5
- (ix) 0·00009251
- (x) $8·985 \times 10^4$

AVERAGES AND AVERAGE SPEED

The average or mean of a set of numbers is the sum of the set divided by the number of members in the set.

$$\text{Average speed} = \frac{\text{Total distance travelled}}{\text{Total time taken}}$$

EXAMPLES

1. The average age of 5 people is 37 years. The average age of 4 of them is 34 years. What is the age of the fifth person?

    Total age of the 5 persons is $37 \times 5 = 185$ years
    Total age of the 4 persons is $34 \times 4 = \underline{136 \text{ years}}$
    Age of fifth person = $\underline{\underline{49 \text{ years}}}$

2. A man cycles 36 km at an average speed of 15 km per hour and then increases his average speed to 22 km per hour for 45 minutes. Find his average speed for the whole journey.

    1st part of journey 15 km travelled in 1 hour

    $$\therefore 36 \text{ km travelled in } \frac{36}{15} \text{ hrs.}$$

    $$= \frac{36}{15} \times 60 \text{ mins.} = 144 \text{ mins.}$$

    2nd part of journey in 60 mins. he travels 22 km

    $$45 \text{ mins. he travels } 22 \times \frac{45}{60} \text{ km} = 16 \cdot 5 \text{ km.}$$

    For whole journey,

    $$\text{total distance travelled} = 16 \cdot 5 \text{ km} + 36 \text{ km} = 52 \cdot 5 \text{ km}$$

    $$\text{total time taken} = 144 \text{ mins} + 45 \text{ mins} = 189 \text{ mins.}$$

    $$= \frac{189}{60} \text{ hrs.}$$

    $$\text{Average speed} = \frac{52 \cdot 5}{\left(\frac{189}{60}\right)} \text{ km per hour}$$

    $$\frac{52 \cdot 5}{189} \times 60 \text{ km per hour}$$

    $$= \frac{3150}{189} = 16 \frac{126}{189} = \underline{\underline{16\tfrac{2}{3} \text{ km per hour}}}$$

PRACTICE QUESTIONS

1. A class of 17 pupils were asked to weigh a lump of lead. 3 of the pupils gave the weight as $21 \cdot 5$g, 7 gave it as $21 \cdot 7$g, 2 gave it as $21 \cdot 4$g, and each of the remaining pupils gave it as $21 \cdot 9$g. What is the average of these weighings, in grammes to 3 s.f?

2. 49 cars of average length 4166mm are parked along the side of a road, the average gap between the cars being 760mm. What length of road, in metres, is occupied by the cars?

3. The average rainfall at a certain place for January, February and March was 1756mm, and for February, March and April was 937mm. If the rainfall in January was 2473mm, find the rainfall in April.

4. The average age of b boys is x years and the average age of g girls is y years. Find the average age of all together.

5. In a class of 26 pupils, the average age of the whole class was 14 years 3 months. One group of 14 pupils in the class had an average age of 14 years 6 months and a further group of 9 pupils had an average age of 13 years 10 months. Find the age of the other 3 pupils if they were all the same age.

6. A car travels from A to B in 54 minutes at an average speed of 119 km per hour. It then travels from B to C at an average speed of 102 km per hour. If the distance from B to C is the same as from A to B find the average speed for the complete journey from A to C, correct to the nearest km per hour.

7. A girl cycles 18 km at an average speed of 30 km per hour and then cycles for the next 20 minutes at an average speed of 36 km per hour. Find the average speed for the whole journey.

8. The money taken by a shop on Monday, Tuesday and Wednesday was £530, £720 and £850 respectively. What was the average daily amount taken? What must the total takings for Friday and Saturday amount to if the average daily takings for the week was £825? (The shop is closed all day on Thursdays.)

9. A train left London at 14.25 and arrived at Cardiff 192 km away at 15.59. Find the average speed for this journey, correct to the nearest km hour^{-1}. After stopping in Cardiff for 12 minutes the train travelled a further 60 km in 48 minutes. What is the average speed for the complete journey including the stop at Cardiff?

FACTORS AND THE REMAINDER THEOREM

FACTORS

To factorise a given expression first extract any **common factor** present, then examine the form of what remains after the extraction of the common factor (if any):

(a) if the expression is a binomial (i.e. two terms) and is the difference of two squares, i.e. of the form $X^2 - Y^2$, then the factors are $(X+Y)(X-Y)$;

(b) if the expression is a trinomial (i.e. three terms) and is of the form $aX^2 + kXY + bY^2$ where a, k, b are numbers then the factors are $(pX + qY)(rX + sY)$ where $a = pr$, $b = qs$ and $k = qr + ps$
(X or Y may be replaced by 1);

(c) if the expression has four terms which may be paired off to give a common factor in the form of a binomial in a bracket, e.g. $ax + bx + ay + by = x(a + b) + y(a + b)$
then the factors are $(a + b)(x + y)$;

(d) if the expression is the sum or difference of two cubes, i.e. has the form $x^3 \pm y^3$,
then the factors are $(x \pm y)(x^2 \mp xy + y^2)$;

(e) if none of the above, the expression may be factorised by making use of the remainder theorem (factor theorem).

EXAMPLE

Factorise the following

(i) $6xy^2 + 4x^2y^3 + 8xy$,
(ii) $a^2 - 4b^2$,
(iii) $2a^2 + 16a + 32$,
(iv) $4a^4 + 36b^2$,
(v) $x^2 - 3xy - 40y^2$,
(vi) $2x^2 + 2xy + xz + zy$.

(i) $6xy^2 + 4x^2y^3 + 8xy$
     $= 2xy(3y + 2xy^2 + 4)$

(ii) $a^2 - 4b^2$
     $= (a + 2b)(a - 4b)$

(iii) $2a^2 + 16a + 32$
     $= 2(a^2 + 8a + 16)$
     $= 2(a + 4)(a + 4)$
     $= 2(a + 4)^2$

(iv) $4a^4 + 36b^2$
     $= 4(a^4 + 9b^2)$

(v) $x^2 - 3xy - 40y^2$
     $= (x - 8y)(x + 5y)$

(vi) $2x^2 + 2xy + xz + zy$
     $= 2x(x + y) + z(x + y)$
     $= (x + y)(2x + z)$

PRACTICE QUESTIONS

1. Factorise
   - (i) $6x - 3x^2$
   - (ii) $b^2 - 7b + 10$
   - (iii) $2x^2 + 5x + 2$
   - (iv) $x^2 - 81$
   - (v) $144 - b^2$
   - (vi) $15cd^2 + 18c^2d$
   - (vii) $cx + dx + cy + dy$
   - (viii) $4a - 4b - xa + xb$
   - (ix) $27 - y^3$
   - (x) $2a^2 + 2b^2$.

2. Factorise the following:
   - (i) $5x^2a^3 + 6x^3a^2$
   - (ii) $9a^2 - b^2$
   - (iii) $8a^2 - 56a + 98$
   - (iv) $2a^3 + 8ab^2$
   - (v) $x^2 - 14xy + 24y^2$
   - (vi) $pqr - r - 2 + 2pq$.

3. Factorise, if possible:
   - (i) $144x^2 - 25y^6$
   - (ii) $144x^2 + y^2$
   - (iii) $x^3 + 64y^3$
   - (iv) $x^3 - 64y^3$.

REMAINDER THEOREM

If P(x), a polynomial in x, is divided by $x - a$ the remainder is P(a).

E.g. $x^2 + 3x + 1 \equiv (x - 1)(x + 4) + 5$

Here $P(x) \equiv x^2 + 3x + 1$ and $x - a = x - 1$ and
$P(1) = 1^2 + 3 \times 1 + 1 = 5$.

To find if $x + 2$ is a factor of $x^3 + 4x^2 + 5x + 2$ we may either divide the polynomial by $x + 2$, thus

$$
\begin{array}{r}
x^2 + 2x + 1 \\
x + 2 \overline{\smash{\big)} x^3 + 4x^2 + 5x + 2} \\
\underline{x^3 + 2x^2 } \\
2x^2 + 5x \\
\underline{2x^2 + 4x } \\
x + 2 \\
\underline{x + 2} \\
0 \quad \text{Rem}
\end{array}
$$

So $x + 2$ is a factor.

Or the Remainder Theorem enables us to determine the remainder directly, thus

$$f(x) \equiv x^3 + 4x^2 + 5x + 2$$
$$f(-2) = (-2)^3 + 4(-2)^2 + 5(-2) + 2$$
$$= -8 + 16 - 10 + 2 = 0, \text{ showing that } x + 2 \text{ is a factor.}$$

(N.B. in $x + 2$, "a" of the theorem is -2.)

PRACTICE QUESTIONS

1(i) Show that $(x + 1)$ is a factor of $x^3 - 4x^2 + x + 6$ and hence find the other two linear factors.

(ii) Find the remainder when $x^3 + 6x^2 - 7x + 8$ is divided by
 (a) $x + 2$ (b) $x - 1$ (c) $3x - 1$.

2. Show that one factor of $x^2 - x + 2$ is a factor of $x^3 - 7x - 6$, and hence find the other factors of the cubic.

3. When the expression $x^3 + 2x^2 + bx - 2$ is divided by $x - 1$ the remainder is -1. Find the value of b.

4. Use the Remainder Theorem to find one factor of $x^3 - 3x^2 - 10x + 24$, and hence factorise the expression completely.

5. Factorise
 (i) $x^3 + 8$ (ii) $125y^3 - b^3$ (iii) $432a^3 - 2b^6$

6. The expression $x^3 + ax^2 + bx - 12$ is exactly divisible by $x - 2$ and $x + 3$. Find the values of a and b and also the remaining factor.

7. Express as the product of four factors,
 (i) $x^4 - 13x^2 + 36$ (ii) $x^6 - y^6$.

8. Determine the values of c and d if $x + 2$ and $x - 3$ are factors of $x^4 + cx^3 - 25x^2 + 26x + d$. Using these values of c and d express $x^4 + cx^2 - 25x^2 + 26x + d$ as the product of four linear factors.

MENSURATION

The reader should be familiar with the following data.

RECTANGLE

Perimeter = 2(l + b) units. Area = lb units^2.

PARALLELOGRAM

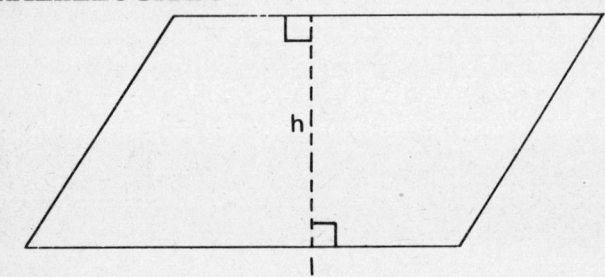

Area = lh units^2.

TRAPEZIUM

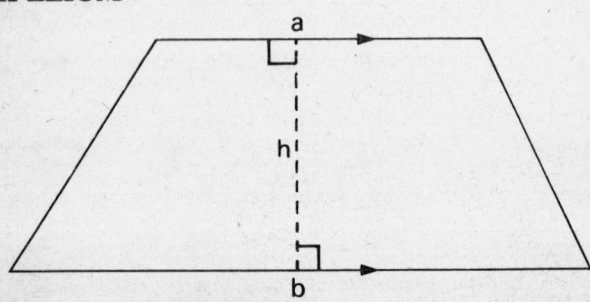

Area = $\frac{1}{2}$ (a + b) h units^2.
I.e. area is $\frac{1}{2}$ × (sum of lengths of parallel sides) × distance between them.

TRIANGLE

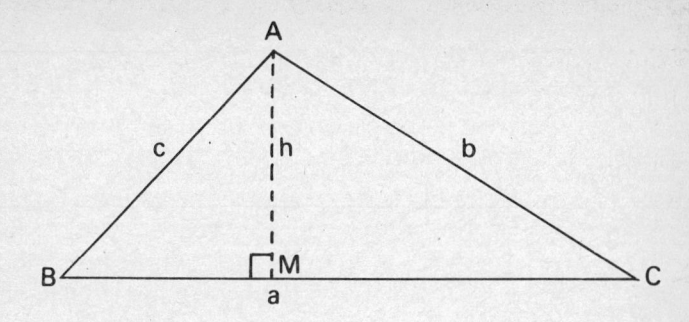

The altitude (or height) corresponding to the base (or side) BC is the perpendicular from A to BC.

(i)   Area of $\triangle$ ABC = $\frac{1}{2} \times$ base $\times$ height
$$= \tfrac{1}{2} \times a \times h \text{ units}^2$$
$$= \tfrac{1}{2} ah \text{ units}^2$$
and similar results when the other sides are taken as base.

(ii)   Area $\triangle$ ABC = $\tfrac{1}{2}$ ab sin C = $\tfrac{1}{2}$ bc sin A = $\tfrac{1}{2}$ ca sin B.

(iii)   Area $\triangle$ ABC = $\sqrt{s(s-a)(s-b)(s-c)}$ where $s = \tfrac{1}{2}(a + b + c)$.

CIRCLE

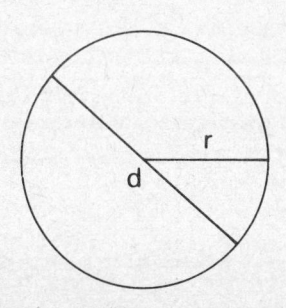

Circumference = π d units
$$= 2\pi r \text{ units.}$$
Area = $\pi r^2 \text{ units}^2$.

CUBOID

Total surface area = 2 (lb + lh + bh) units^2.
Volume = lbh units^3.

CIRCULAR CYLINDER

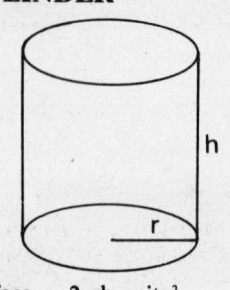

Area of curved surface = 2πrh units^2.
Volume = πr^2h units^3.
Total surface area of a solid cylinder = 2πrh + 2πr^2
                                      = 2πr (h + r) units^2.

CIRCULAR CONE

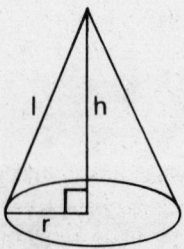

Area of curved surface = πrl units^2.
Volume = $\frac{1}{3}\pi r^2$h units^3.

PYRAMIDS

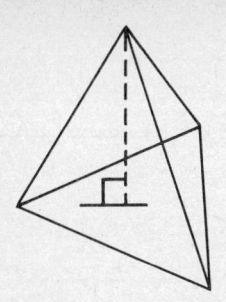

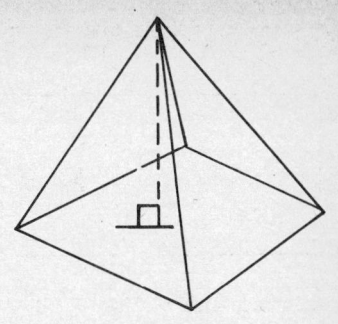

Volume = $\frac{1}{3}$ × area of the base × perpendicular height.

SPHERE

Radius r
Area of surface = $4\pi r^2$ units^2.
Volume = $\frac{4}{3}\pi r^3$ units^3.

EXAMPLES

1. There is an average depth of 7·5cm of snow on a flat rectangular field whose length is 160m and breadth is 65m. If 1cm^3 of snow weighs 0·085g, calculate in tonnes the weight of snow on the field (1 tonne = 1000kg).

    Volume of snow = 16000 × 6500 × 7·5cm^3
    $\qquad\qquad\qquad$ = 16 × 65 × 75 × 10^{4}cm^3
    $\qquad\qquad\qquad$ = 7800 × 10^{4}cm^3
    $\qquad\qquad\qquad$ = 78 × 10^{6}cm^3
    Weight of snow = 78 × 10^6 × 0·085g
    $\qquad\qquad\qquad$ = 78 × 0·085 tonnes
    $\qquad\qquad\qquad$ = <u>6·63 tonnes</u>

2. The minute hand of a clock is 3·5cm long. For the period between 12.15 p.m. and 12.40 p.m. calculate
    (a) the distance through which the tip of the hand travels,
    (b) the angle through which the hand rotates,
    (c) the area swept over by the hand. (Take $\pi = \frac{22}{7}$ and give answer to (a) and (c) correct to 1 decimal place.)
    12.15 p.m. to 12.40 p.m. is 25 mins.

(a) tip of hand travels $\frac{25}{60} \times 2\pi r$
$= \frac{25}{60} \times 2 \times \frac{22}{7} \times 3\cdot 5$ cm
$= \frac{55}{6}$ cm
$= 9\frac{1}{6}$ cm
$= 9\cdot 16$ cm
$= \underline{9\cdot 2\text{cm to 1 decimal place}}$

(b) Angle hand rotates $= \frac{25}{60} \times 360°$
$= \underline{150°}$

(c) Area swept over $= \frac{25}{60} \times \pi r^2$
$= \frac{5}{12} \times \frac{22}{7} \times 3\cdot 5 \times 3\cdot 5$ cm^2
$= \frac{192\cdot 5}{12}$ cm^2
$= 16\cdot 04$ cm^2
$= \underline{16\cdot 0\text{cm}^2 \text{ to 1 decimal place}}$

3. Find the area of the curved surface and the volume of a cone whose height is 16cm and base diameter 24cm. (Take $\pi = 3\cdot 14$.)

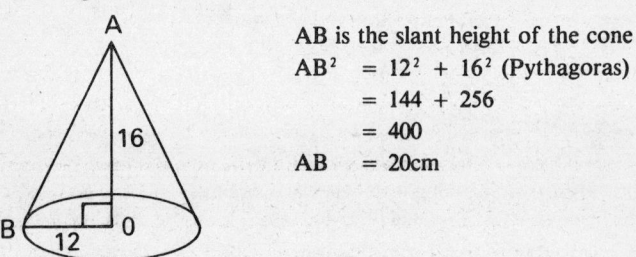

AB is the slant height of the cone
$AB^2 = 12^2 + 16^2$ (Pythagoras)
$= 144 + 256$
$= 400$
$AB = 20$ cm

Area of curved surface of cone $= \pi rl$
$= 3\cdot 14 \times 12 \times 20$ cm^2
$= \underline{753\cdot 6\text{cm}^2}$

Vol. of cone $= \frac{1}{3}\pi r^2 h$
$= \frac{1}{3} \times 3\cdot 14 \times 144 \times 16$ cm^3
$= 3\cdot 14 \times 48 \times 16$ cm^3
$= \underline{2411\cdot 5\text{cm}^3}$

PRACTICE QUESTIONS

Give answers correct to 3 s.f. Take $\pi = 3\cdot 142$ unless stated otherwise.

1(a) Concrete is to be placed to a depth of 120mm on a flat rectangular yard 15m by 28m. Calculate the volume of concrete required, in m^3.

1(b) Find the weight, in grams, of a cylindrical metal bar 3·45dm long and with diameter 4·7cm, if the metal weighs 7·45g per cm^3.

2. The hour hand of a clock is 7·5cm long. Find:
   (a) the angle through which it turns;
   (b) the distance through which the tip of the hand travels;
   (c) the area swept over by the hand;
   for the period between 7 a.m. and 4 p.m.

3. Find (a) the total surface area; and, (b) the volume of a cone whose diameter is 17·5cm and height 28·4cm.

4. Find the area of a ring bounded by two concentric circles of diameter 134mm and 123mm respectively.

5. A cylindrical metal pipe 5m long has an internal diameter of 20cm and an external diameter of 24cm. Calculate the weight in kilogrammes of the pipe given that the density of the metal in the pipe is 8·5g per cm^3.

6. A hemispherical bowl with internal radius 10cm, full of water, is emptied into an empty cylindrical vessel with internal radius 4cm. Find the depth of water in the vessel.

7. The external diameter of a hollow metal sphere is 14cm and the thickness of the metal is 1·75cm. The sphere is melted down and recast as a solid circular cylinder of diameter 13·25cm. Find the height of the cylinder.

8. An empty rectangular tank has a horizontal rectangular base 15cm by 20cm and vertical sides height 1m. A heavy solid cone is placed upright in the tank. Water is poured into the tank until the apex of the cone is just covered. If the height of the cone is 25cm and base diameter is 8cm find the volume of water poured into the tank.
   When the cone is removed find by what amount the water level falls.

9. The diagram on p.30 shows the net of a square based pyramid and consists of a square of side 10cm and 4 congruent isosceles triangles of height 13cm. Calculate:
   (a) the height of the pyramid;
   (b) the volume of the pyramid;

10cm

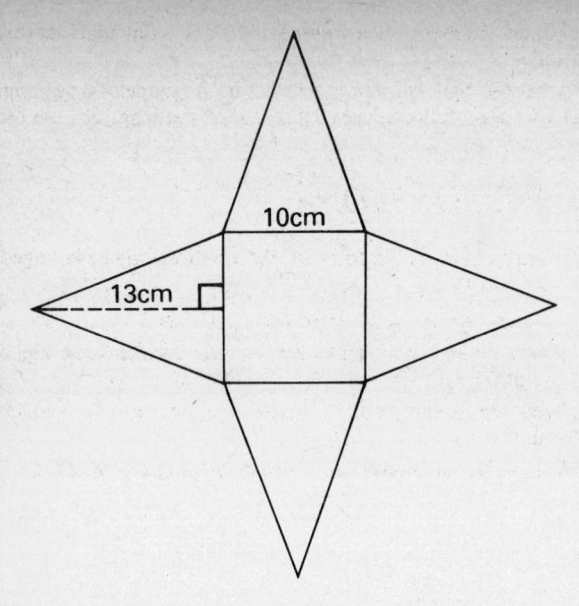

13cm

(c) the angle which a triangular face makes with the base of the pyramid;
(d) total surface area of the pyramid.

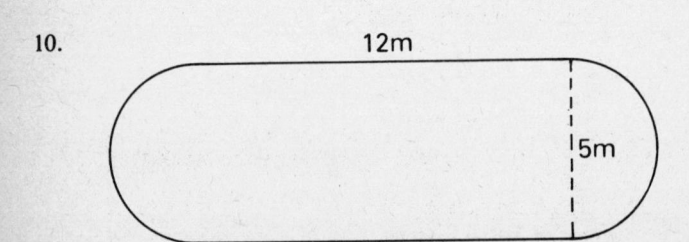

10.   12m

5m

The diagram above shows a lawn consisting of a rectangular middle 12m by 5m with two semi-circular ends. The lawn is to be surrounded by a concrete path 1·5m wide and 100mm deep.

Find, in m³, the volume of concrete needed.

If a builder charges 75p per m² for constructing the path what will his total bill be (to nearest p.)?

11. A solid metal sphere has a volume of $14\frac{1}{3}$cm³. Calculate its surface area (take $\pi = \frac{22}{7}$).

The sphere is melted down and recast in the shape of a rectangular block of cross-sectional area $2\frac{1}{4}$cm². Find the length of the block.

LINEAR EQUATIONS

When solving an equation the form of the equation may be changed by:
  (i) adding the same term to each side;
  (ii) subtracting the same term from each side;
  (iii) multiplying every term on each side by the same algebraic number;
  (iv) dividing every term on each side by the same algebraic number.

The use of these laws is illustrated in the following examples.

EXAMPLES

1. Solve the equations

   (i) $3(x + 2) = 4 - (2 - x)$ (ii) $\frac{3x}{5} - \frac{x-2}{15} = 2$

   (i)
   $$3(x + 2) = 4 - (2 - x)$$
   $$6x + 6 = 4 - 2 + x$$
   $$6x - x + 6 = 2 + x - x$$
   $$5x + 6 - 6 = 2 - 6$$
   $$5x = -4$$
   $$\underline{x = -\tfrac{4}{5}}$$

   (ii) $\frac{3x}{5} - \frac{(x-2)}{15} = 2$ (NB the inclusion of the bracket)

   Multiply both sides by 15
   $$9x - (x - 2) = 30$$
   $$9x - x + 2 = 30$$
   $$8x = 30 - 2$$
   $$8x = 28$$
   $$x = \frac{28}{8}$$
   $$\underline{x = 3\tfrac{1}{2}}$$

2. Solve the equations for x

   (i) $\dfrac{x+5}{x-1} = \dfrac{x+2}{x-3}$ (ii) $5(2p + x) = 4(ax + p)$

   (i) $\dfrac{x+5}{x-1} = \dfrac{x+2}{x-3}$

   Multiply both sides by $(x-1)(x-3)$
   $$(x+5)(x-3) = (x+2)(x-1)$$
   $$x^2 + 3x - 15 = x^2 + x - 2$$
   $$2x = 13$$

   (ii) $\quad 5(2p + x) = 4(ax + p)$
   $$10p + 5x = 4ax + 4p$$
   $$5x - 4ax = -6p$$
   $$x(5 - 4a) = -6p$$
   $$x = \dfrac{-6p}{5 - 4a}$$
   $$x = \dfrac{6p}{4a - 5}$$

PRACTICE QUESTIONS

1. Solve the equations:
   (i) $8x - 3 = 21$ (ii) $4x + 5 = 7x - 13$
   (iii) $\dfrac{3x}{2} = 6$ (iv) $\dfrac{x}{3} - \dfrac{x}{4} = 2$

2. Solve the following equations and verify the solutions,
   (i) $2 - (3 - x) = 5$ (ii) $5(2x - 3) = 10$
   (iii) $\dfrac{x+1}{2} + 5 = x$ (iv) $\tfrac{3}{4}(x + 2) = 6$

3. Multiply,
   (i) $2x + 3$ by $2x - 3$ and   (ii) $4x - 1$ and $x - 2$
   Hence solve the equation,
   $(2x + 3)(2x - 3) = (4x - 1)(x - 2) + 7$

4. Solve the equations,
   (i) $7(x + 4) = 6 - (4 - x)$ (ii) $\dfrac{3x}{4} - \dfrac{x-4}{8} = 3$

5. Solve the equation for x,
   (i) $\dfrac{x-3}{x-1} = \dfrac{x+4}{x+1}$
   (ii) $3(4p + x) = 2(bx - p)$

6. Solve the equations for x,
   (i) $\dfrac{5(2x-1)}{4} - \dfrac{3(x-1)}{6} = 1\tfrac{1}{2}$
   (ii) $3ax - \dfrac{2x}{c} = 3c$

7. Find the value of x if, $\dfrac{x-3}{6} + \dfrac{5-2x}{4} = 5 - \dfrac{8+x}{2}$

8. Find the value of y when,
   (i) $3(2 - y) - 8(4y + 2) = 7 - 2(7y - 2)$
   (ii) $\dfrac{8 + y^2}{y} = y + 4$

9. Solve the equation, $(x - 3)(x + 2) = 7(x - 5) + x(x - 3) - 6$.

10. Find x in terms of a and b if,
    (i) $3x + a = b$
    (ii) $a - (x + 3b) = 4$
    (iii) $3x + 2 = ax + b$
    (iv) $(x + a)^2 = 4b^2$.

PROBLEMS INVOLVING LINEAR EQUATIONS

Read the question carefully. Decide what you are given and what you are asked to find. Choose a letter to stand for the unknown number which the question asks you to find. If the problem involves quantities state your units carefully.

State precisely what your chosen letter represents e.g. let speed of car be x km per hour, or let cost of the articles be £y, or let the larger number be n.

The question will contain statements which will enable you to write down two different expressions for the same thing and thus you form your equation containing your unknown. After solving your equation check your answer by using the data as given in the question, not just by substituting in the equation which you have formed as this equation may be incorrect.

Always end your solution with a statement explaining what you have found.

EXAMPLES

1. Twenty books cost a total of £70. Some cost £2 each and the rest £4.50 each. How many of the cheaper books were bought?

   Let the number of cheaper books bought be x.

   Then the number of dearer books bought is $(20 - x)$.

   Cost of cheaper books was £2x.

   Cost of dearer books was £$4\frac{1}{2}$. $(20 - x)$.

   Total cost was £2x + £$4\frac{1}{2}(20 - x)$.

   But total cost was £70.

   $\therefore 2x + 4\frac{1}{2}(20 - x) = 70.$

   $2x + 90 - 4\frac{1}{2}x = 70.$

   $-2\frac{1}{2}x = -20$

   $\frac{1}{2}x = 20$

   $x = 20 \times \frac{2}{5} = 8$

   ∴ <u>8 cheaper books were bought</u>

   <u>Check</u> with data in question. £2 × 8 + £4.50 × 12 =
   £16 + £54 = <u>£70</u>✓

2. A man completed a journey of 470km in 7 hours. He travelled partly at an average speed of 60km per hour and partly at an average speed of 80km per hour. How long did he travel at the average speed of 80km per hour?

   Let the man travel at the average speed of 80km per hour for h hours.

   Then he travelled at an average speed of 60km per hour for $(7 - h)$ hours.

   Distance travelled in h hours is 80h km.

   Distance travelled in $(7 - h)$ hours if $60(7 - h)$ km.

   Total distance travelled is $80h + 60(7 - h)$ kms.

   But total distance travelled is 470km.

   $\therefore 80h + 60(7 - h) = 470$

   $80h + 420 - 60h = 470$

   $20h = 50$

   $h = \frac{50}{20} = 2\frac{1}{2}$

   ∴ <u>He travelled at an average speed of 80km per hour for $2\frac{1}{2}$ hours.</u>

   <u>Check.</u> $2\frac{1}{2}$ hours at 80km per hour = 200km

   $7 - 2\frac{1}{2} = 4\frac{1}{2}$ hours at 60km per hour = 270km

   Total distance = 470km

PRACTICE QUESTIONS

1. Thirty books cost a total of £51. Some cost £1.50 each and the rest cost £2 each. How many of the cheaper books were bought?

2. A man completed a journey of 390km in 4 hours 45 min. He travelled partly at an average speed of 70km per hour and partly at an average speed of 100km per hour. How long did he travel at the average speed of 100km per hour?

3. A girl cycled from her home to the local library at 24km per hour. She stayed $\frac{1}{4}$ hour at the library and then returned home, cycling at 20km per hour. She was away from home for $72\frac{1}{2}$ minutes. How far was the library from her home?

4. One regular polygon has half the number of sides of a second regular polygon. The size of each interior angle of the first polygon is $\frac{3}{4}$ the size of each interior angle of the second polygon.

   How many sides has the first polygon?

5. A girl starts to walk to school at 8 a.m. walking at a steady speed of 3km/hour. Half an hour later her brother starts to cycle to the same school at a steady speed of 12km/hour. When and where does the brother overtake his sister?

QUADRATIC EQUATIONS

An equation with at least one term of degree two is called a quadratic equation, e.g. $3x^2 + x = 5$, since $3x^2$ is of degree 2 in x.

There are two general methods of solution.

The first depends on the fact that if the product of a finite number of factors is zero, then at least one of the factors must be zero. The first step in the method is to bring all the terms to one side of the equation, leaving a zero on the other side. Now factorise the terms. Since they are equated to zero, one factor must be zero,

e.g. To solve the equation $x^2 - x = 2$:

$$x^2 - x = 2$$
$$x^2 - x - 2 = 0$$
$$(x - 2)(x + 1) = 0$$

Either $x - 2 = 0$ or $x + 1 = 0$

$$\underline{x = 2 \text{ or } x = -1}$$

In the second method the terms containing the unknown are placed on one side of the equation and the constant (number only) term on the other side. The coefficient of the second degree term is made 1 (if it is not so already), and then the process of "completing the square" is performed making the expression in the unknown into a perfect square. The square root of both sides is then taken and leads to the solution.

EXAMPLES

1. Solve the equation $2x^2 = 5 - 9x$.

$$2x^2 = 5 - 9x$$
$$2x^2 + 9x = 5$$
$$x^2 + \tfrac{9}{2}x = \tfrac{5}{2}$$
$$x^2 + \tfrac{9}{2}x + (\tfrac{9}{4})^2 = \tfrac{5}{2} + (\tfrac{9}{4})^2, \text{ completing the square}$$
$$(x + \tfrac{9}{4})^2 = \tfrac{121}{16}$$
$$x + \tfrac{9}{4} = \pm\tfrac{11}{4} \text{ taking square roots.}$$

Either $x + \tfrac{9}{4} = \tfrac{11}{4}$ or $x + \tfrac{9}{4} = -\tfrac{11}{4}$
$$x = \tfrac{2}{4} \text{ or } x = -\tfrac{20}{4}$$
i.e. $\underline{x = \tfrac{1}{2} \text{ or } -5}$

N.B. This equation could have been solved using the first method.

The advantage of the second method is that it can be used when the first method fails because the expression obtained by placing all terms on one side of the equation will not factorise. In this case the second method will lead to an answer which may be approximated to a given degree of accuracy.

2. Solve the equation $6y^2 - 7y - 2 = 0$, giving the roots correct to 1 decimal place.

$$6y^2 - 7y - 2 = 0$$

There are no factors to $6y^2 - 7y - 2$.

Hence re-write the equation as,

$$6y^2 - 7y = 2$$
$$y^2 - \frac{7}{6}y = \frac{1}{3}$$
$$y^2 - \frac{7}{6}y + \left(\frac{7}{12}\right)^2 = \frac{1}{3} + \left(\frac{7}{12}\right)^2$$
$$\left(y - \frac{7}{12}\right)^2 = \frac{1}{3} + \frac{49}{144}$$
$$\left(y - \frac{7}{12}\right)^2 = \frac{97}{144}$$
$$y - \frac{7}{12} = \sqrt{\frac{97}{144}}$$

$$y - \frac{7}{12} = \pm \frac{\sqrt{97}}{12}$$

Either $y - \frac{7}{12} = \frac{\sqrt{97}}{12}$ or $y - \frac{7}{12} = -\frac{\sqrt{97}}{12}$

$y = \frac{9 \cdot 849}{12} + \frac{7}{12}$ or $y = -\frac{9 \cdot 849}{12} + \frac{7}{12}$

$y = \frac{16 \cdot 849}{12}$ or $y = -\frac{2 \cdot 849}{12}$

$y = 1 \cdot 40$ or $y = -0 \cdot 23$

$\underline{y = 1 \cdot 4 \text{ or } -0 \cdot 2 \text{ correct to 1 decimal place}}$

The "completing the square" method when applied to the general quadratic equation

$$ax^2 + bx + c = 0$$

gives rise to a formula for writing down its roots—

$$x = \frac{-b \pm \sqrt{b^2 - 4ac}}{2a}$$

This formula may be used instead of the process of "completing the square".

3. Solve, giving the roots correct to 2.s.f., the equation,

$2x^2 - 5x = 4.$

$2x^2 - 5x - 4 = 0$

$a = 2, b = -5\ c = -4$ in

$$x = \frac{-b \pm \sqrt{b^2 - 4ac}}{2a}$$

$$x = \frac{5 \pm \sqrt{25 - 4(2)(-4)}}{4}$$

$$= \frac{5 \pm \sqrt{25 + 32}}{4}$$

$$= \frac{5 \pm \sqrt{57}}{4}$$

$$= \frac{5 \pm 7 \cdot 550}{4}$$

Either $x = \dfrac{5 + 7\cdot550}{4}$ or $x = \dfrac{5 - 7\cdot550}{4}$

$x = \dfrac{12\cdot550}{4}$ or $x = -\dfrac{2\cdot550}{4}$

$x = 3\cdot13$ or $x = -0\cdot637$

$\therefore \underline{x = 3\cdot1 \text{ or } -0\cdot64 \text{ to 2 s.f.}}$

PRACTICE QUESTIONS

1. Solve
   (i) $x^2 = 196$
   (ii) $(x + 3)^2 = 289$
   (iii) $y^2 - 8y + 12 = 0$
   (iv) $3x^2 = 7x + 6$

2. Solve
   (i) $2(1 - Z^2) = 3Z$
   (ii) $(2x + 1)^2 = 9x^2$
   (iii) $(2y + 3)(y + 1) = (y + 2)^2 + 5$

3. Solve, giving the answers correct to 3 s.f.
   (i) $2x^2 - 3x - 7 = 0$
   (ii) $Z^2 = 2(5 - 4Z)$

4. Solve the following equations, if the roots are irrational give the answers correct to 2 decimal places.
   (i) $9x(2x - 1) = 5$
   (ii) $(3x + 1)(x - 2) + x(5x + 6) = 0$
   (iii) $(2x + 3)(x - 4) + 24 = 2(3x - 1)(x - 1)$
   (iv) $3(x - 4) + (4x - 3)(8x + 5) = 1 + 3x$
   (v) $9x(x - 4) + 2 = 3(x - 11)$

PROBLEMS INVOLVING QUADRATIC EQUATIONS

The techniques stated in Problems involving linear equations (page 33) still apply. When the equation which has to be solved is quadratic, both roots of the equation do not necessarily give solutions to the given problem. It is therefore very important to check whether each root actually satisfies the conditions given in the problem.

EXAMPLES

1. Twenty-six years hence a person's age will be the square of what it was 30 years ago.

Find the person's present age.

Let the person's present age be x years

26 years hence the person's age will be (x + 26) years

30 years ago the person's age was (x − 30) years

$$\therefore \quad x + 26 = (x - 30)^2$$
$$x + 26 = x^2 - 60x + 900$$
$$0 = x^2 - 61x + 874$$
$$0 = (x - 38)(x - 23)$$

Either x − 38 = 0 or x − 23 = 0

x = 38 or x = 23.

Check   (i) Let person's age now be 38 years

26 years hence age will be 64 years

30 years ago age was 8 years

and $64 = 8^2$.

(ii) Let person's age now be 23 years

30 years ago no age. So this root of the equation does not satisfy the conditions in the problem.

Hence: <u>The person is 38 years old now.</u>

2. Find two consecutive integers such that the sum of their squares is 421.

Let the smaller integer be y.

Then the larger integer is (y + 1).

The sum of their squares is $y^2 + (y + 1)^2$.

$$\therefore \quad y^2 + (y + 1)^2 = 421$$
$$y^2 + y^2 + 2y + 1 = 421$$
$$2y^2 + 2y - 420 = 0$$
$$y^2 + y - 210 = 0$$
$$(y + 15)(y - 14) = 0$$

Either y = − 15 or y = 14

∴ <u>The integers are either − 15 and − 14 or 14 and 15.</u>

PRACTICE QUESTIONS

1. Thirty-six years hence a person's age will be the square of what it was thirty-six years ago.

What is his present age?

2. Two adjacent sides of a rectangle differ by 7m. The area of the rectangle is 98m². Find its length.

3. The square of a number minus five times the number equals eighty-four. What is the number?

4. Find two consecutive odd integers such that twice the square of the smaller equals eleven times the larger plus ninety-nine.

5. A train travelled 48km at xkm per hour and 240km at (x + 12)km per hour. The average speed for the 288km was 57·6km per hour. Find x.

SIMULTANEOUS EQUATIONS (LINEAR IN TWO UNKNOWNS)

If we have a single equation in two unknowns we can find an infinite number of pairs of values of the unknowns which satisfy it.
E.g. $2x + y = 4$ when $(x = 0, y = 4)$, $(x = 1\ y = 2)$, $(x = -1\ y = 6)$ etc.
Again $3x - y = 11$ when $(x = 0\ y = -11)$, $(x = 1, y = -8)$, $(x = 4\ y = 1)$ etc.
But if $2x + y = 4$ and $3x - y = 11$ simultaneously then there is only one pair of values $(x = 3, y = -2)$ which satisfies both equations.

There are various methods for obtaining the solution to such simultaneous equations as illustrated in the following examples.

EXAMPLES

1. Solve the simultaneous equations $x - 2y = 6$ and $2x + 3y = 5$.

   $x - 2y = 6$ **1**
   $2x + 3y = 5$ **2**

   From equation **1** $x = 6 + 2y$

   Substitute in equation **2**

   $2(6 + 2y) + 3y = 5$
   $12 + 4y + 3y = 5$
   $7y = -7$
   $y = -1$

   Substitute $y = -1$ in **1**, $x + 2 = 6$
   $x = 4$.

   $\therefore \underline{x = 4, y = -1}$

   Check Substitute $x = 4, y = -1$ in = LHS of **1**
   $4 - 2(-1) = 6 = $ RHS of **1**
   and in LHS of **2**
   $8 + 3(-1) = 5 = $ RHS of **2**

2. Solve the simultaneous equations
$2x - 5y = 11$ and $3x + 2y = -12$.
$$2x - 5y = 11 \quad \mathbf{1}$$
$$3x + 2y = -12 \quad \mathbf{2}$$

Multiply eqn. **1** by 3 and eqn. **2** by 2
$$6x - 15y = 33$$
$$6x + 4y = -24$$

Subtract $-19y = 57$
$$y = -3$$

Substitute $y = -3$ in eqn. **1**
$$2x + 15 = 11$$
$$2x = -4$$
$$x = -2.$$
$\therefore \underline{(x = -2, y = -3)}$

N.B. Check that this pair of values satisfies both original eqns.

3. Solve the simultaneous equations
$$4x + 5y = 22 \quad \mathbf{1}$$
$$3x - 2y = 5 \quad \mathbf{2}$$

Equations **1** and **2** are represented by the single matrix equation.
$$\begin{pmatrix} 4 & 5 \\ 3 & -2 \end{pmatrix} \begin{pmatrix} x \\ y \end{pmatrix} = \begin{pmatrix} 22 \\ 5 \end{pmatrix}$$

The inverse of $\begin{pmatrix} 4 & 5 \\ 3 & -2 \end{pmatrix}$ is $-\dfrac{1}{23}\begin{pmatrix} -2 & -5 \\ -3 & 4 \end{pmatrix}$

Hence
$$\begin{pmatrix} x \\ y \end{pmatrix} = -\frac{1}{23}\begin{pmatrix} -2 & -5 \\ -3 & 4 \end{pmatrix}\begin{pmatrix} 22 \\ 5 \end{pmatrix}$$
$$= -\frac{1}{23}\begin{pmatrix} -69 \\ -46 \end{pmatrix}$$
$$= \begin{pmatrix} 3 \\ 2 \end{pmatrix}$$

$\therefore \underline{x = 3, y = 2}$

The method which a student will use is his own choice. Remember to check your solution in both of the original equations.

PRACTICE QUESTIONS

Solve the following simultaneous equations,

1. $x + y = 7$
   $3x - y = 9$

2. $5x + 4y = 4$
   $3x + 2y = 0$

3. $3x + 2y = 6$
   $6x + 3y = 9\frac{1}{2}$

4. $2x + 5y = -11$
   $3x - 10y = 36$

5. $4(x + y) = \frac{1}{2}(14x - y) = -5.$

6. $3x - y = 10 - 2x + y = 14 - x.$

7. $4x - 5y - 13 = 0.$
   $6x + 7y + 53 = 0.$

SIMULTANEOUS EQUATIONS (1 LINEAR 1 QUADRATIC)

The general method of solution is to use the linear equation to obtain one unknown in terms of the other and substitute this result in the quadratic equation thus eliminating one unknown and obtaining a quadratic equation in one unknown. Substitute each root of this equation in the derived linear equation to obtain the two pairs of roots.

EXAMPLE

Solve the simultaneous equations
$$x - y = 2$$
$$x^2 + 3x + y^2 - 7 = 0$$

$$x - y = 2 \quad \mathbf{1}$$
$$x^2 + 3x + y^2 - 7 = 0 \quad \mathbf{2}$$

From eqn. **1** $y = x - 2$ **3** Substitute in eqn. **2**
$$x^2 + 3x + (x - 2)^2 - 7 = 0$$
$$x^2 + 3x + x^2 - 4x + 4 - 7 = 0$$
$$2x^2 - x - 3 = 0$$
$$(2x - 3)(x + 1) = 0$$

Either $2x - 3 = 0$ or $x + 1 = 0$
$$x = 1\frac{1}{2} \quad \text{or} \quad x = -1$$

Substitute $x = 1\frac{1}{2}$ in eqn. **3**
$$y = 1\frac{1}{2} - 2 = \frac{1}{2}.$$

Substitute $x = -1$ in eqn. **3**
$$y = -1 - 2 = -3$$
$\therefore$ $\underline{(x = 1\frac{1}{2}, y = -\frac{1}{2}) \text{ or } (x = -1, y = -3)}$

<u>Check</u> Substitute $x = 1\frac{1}{2}, y = -\frac{1}{2}$ in the LHS of eqn. **1** and eqn. **2**
$$1\frac{1}{2} - (-\frac{1}{2}) = 2 \text{ RHS of eqn. } \mathbf{1}$$
$$2\frac{1}{4} + 4\frac{1}{2} + (-\frac{1}{2})^2 - 7$$
$$= 2\frac{1}{4} + 4\frac{1}{2} + \frac{1}{4} - 7 = 0 = \text{RHS of } \mathbf{2}$$

Substitute $x = -1, y = -3$ in LHS of eqn. **1** and eqn. **2**
$$-1 + 3 = 2 = \text{RHS of eqn. } \mathbf{1}$$
$$1 - 3 + 9 - 7 = 0 = \text{RHS of eqn. } \mathbf{2}$$

PRACTICE QUESTIONS

Solve the following simultaneous equations.

1. $x + 2y = -1$
   $x^2 - 2xy - 8y = 7$

2. $x + y = 1$
   $x^2 + y^2 - y = 15$

3. $3x + 2y = 10$
   $3xy - 7y + 5 = 0$

4. $9y - 2x - 7 = 0$
   $2x^2 + 27y^2 - 21y - 4 = 0$

PROBLEMS INVOLVING SIMULTANEOUS EQUATIONS

As with all problems, read the question carefully. Decide what you are given and what you have to find. If the problem involves two unknowns choose two letters to stand for the unknown numbers of these unknowns. State the units connected with the unknown numbers. The question will contain information which will enable you to form two equations in the unknowns which hold simultaneously. Solve these and write down the final statement of your answer.

Check your answer against the information given in the question.

EXAMPLE

A certain number, of two digits, is six times the sum of its digits. It is also 9 more than the number formed by interchanging the digits.
Find the number.

Let the tens digit be t and the units digit be u.
Then the number is $(10t + u)$.

The sum of its digits is $(t + u)$

$$\therefore (10t + u) = 6(t + u)$$
$$10t + u = 6t + 6u$$
$$4t - 5u = 0 \quad \mathbf{1}$$

The number formed by interchanging the digits is $(10u + t)$.

$$\therefore (10t + u) = (10u + t) + 9$$
$$10t + u = 10u + t + 9$$
$$9t - 9u = 9$$
$$t - u = 1 \quad \mathbf{2}$$

Substitute $t = 1 + u$ for t in **1**
$$4(1 + u) - 5u = 0$$
$$4 + 4u - 5u = 0$$
$$4 = u$$
$$\therefore t = 1 + 4 = 5$$

∴ The number is 54.

The reader is left to see that this answer agrees with the data in question.

PRACTICE QUESTIONS

1. A certain two-digit number is 4 times the sum of its digits. It is also 27 less than the number formed by interchanging the digits.
   Find the number.

2. A bag of coins consists of 10p pieces and 50p pieces. There are 19 coins in the bag with a total value of £6.30.
   Find how many coins of each kind there are in the bag.

3. The cost of 1kg of strawberries is 10p more than four times the cost of 1kg of apples. The product of the numbers of pence in the cost per kg of these fruit is 15,000.
   Find the cost per kg of the fruits.

4. If 1 is subtracted from the numerator of a fraction and 2 is added to the denominator the new fraction so formed reduces to $\frac{1}{3}$. If 2 is added to the numerator and 1 is added to the denominator of the original fraction the new fraction so formed reduces to $\frac{3}{4}$.
   Find the original fraction.

5. Two years ago a man was eight times as old as his son. In three years time he will be four and a half times his son's age then.
   How old are they now?

GRAPHS

LINEAR FUNCTIONS AND STRAIGHT LINE GRAPHS

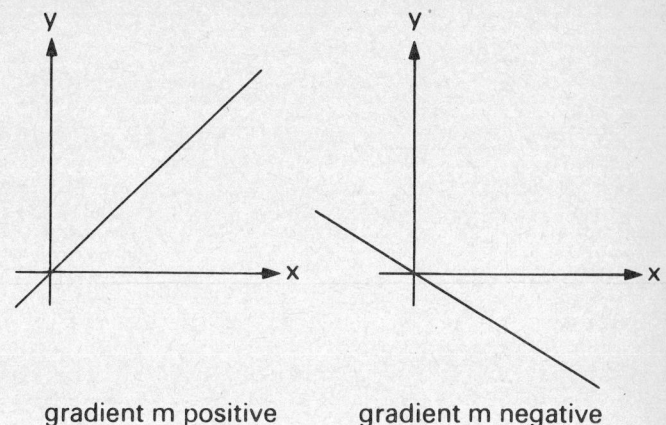

gradient m positive   gradient m negative

The equation of a straight line passing through the origin and with gradient m is,

$$y = mx$$

$$\text{or } \frac{y}{x} = m$$

We say that y is proportional to x or that y varies (directly) as x.

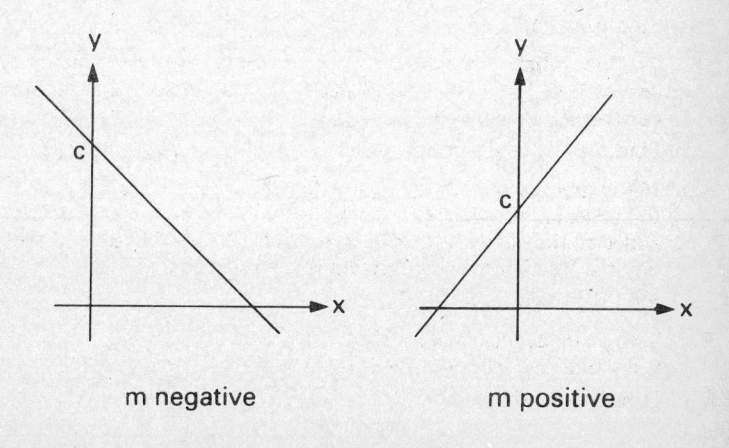

m negative   m positive

The equation of the line with gradient m passing through (o, c) is,
$$y = mx + c$$
The equation of the line with gradient m passing through (x_1, y_1) is,
$$y - y_1 = m(x - x_1)$$

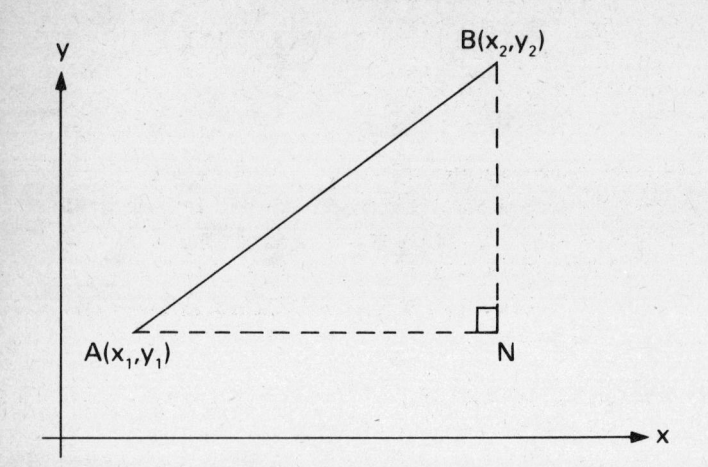

If **A** is the point (x_1, y_1) and **B** is the point (x_2, y_2) then
(i) the **length AB** is $\sqrt{(x_2 - x_1)^2 + (y_2 - y_1)^2}$ (which is obtained by using Pythagoras' theorem in $\triangle$ ABN).

(ii) the **gradient** of **AB** is $\dfrac{y_2 - y_1}{x_2 - x_1}$

(iii) the equation of AB is $y - y_1 = \dfrac{y_2 - y_1}{x_2 - x_1}(x - x_1)$

this is sometimes rewritten as $\dfrac{y - y_1}{x - x_1} = \dfrac{y_2 - y_1}{x_2 - x_1}$

EXAMPLE

The coordinates of P are $(-2, 6)$ and of Q are $(8, -8)$. Calculate (a) the length of PQ (b) the gradient of PQ (c) the equation of PQ.

(a) $(PQ)^2 = [8 - (-2)]^2 + [-8 - 6]^2$
$= 10^2 + (-14)^2$
$= 100 + 196 = 296$
PQ $= \sqrt{296} = \underline{17 \cdot 2}$ to 3 s.f.

EITHER

(b) gradient of PQ = $\dfrac{-8-6}{8-(-2)} = \dfrac{-14}{10} = \underline{-1\cdot 4}$

(c) equation of PQ is $y - 6 = -1\cdot 4\,[x - (-2)]$
multiplying both sides by 5
$5y - 30 = -7(x + 2)$
$5y - 30 = -7x - 14$
so eqn. of PQ is $\underline{7x + 5y - 16 = 0}$

OR

Let the equation of PQ be $\qquad y = mx + c.$
Since P $(-2,6)$ lies on the line $\qquad 6 = -2m + c$ **1**
and since Q $(8, -8)$ lies on the line $\quad -8 = 8m + c$ **2**
Subtracting **2** from **1** $\qquad 14 = -10m$
$\qquad\qquad\qquad\qquad\qquad\qquad \therefore \underline{m = -1\cdot 4}$
Substitute in **1** $\qquad\qquad 6 = 2\cdot 8 + c$
$\qquad\qquad\qquad\qquad\qquad\qquad +3\cdot 2 = c$
the equation of PQ is $\qquad y = -1\cdot 4x + 3\cdot 2$
multiply both sides by 5
$\qquad\qquad\qquad\qquad\qquad\qquad 5y = -7x + 16$
$\qquad\qquad\qquad\underline{7x + 5y - 16 = 0}$

PRACTICE QUESTIONS

1. Find the length of the line AB when A is the point (2,4) and B is the point (5,8).

2. Calculate the equation of the line passing through $(-4,7)$ with a gradient of $-\tfrac{2}{3}$.

3. On graph paper draw x and y axes for values of x and y from 0 to 10. Take 1cm as unit on each axis.
   (a) Plot the points A (2,3), B(6,4) and D(4,5). Join AB and AD. Plot the point C which makes ABCD a parallelogram. Write down the coordinates of C.
   (b) Calculate the equation of AC and deduce the coordinates of the point where CA produced cuts the y-axis. Verify your result by drawing CA produced on your graph.

DISTANCE-TIME GRAPHS

If a car travels at a uniform speed (i.e. a constant or steady speed) of u km per hour the distance s km travelled in t hours is given by

$$s = ut$$

In this case the distance-time graph is thus a straight line.

EXAMPLE

A man starts from home at noon and travels at a uniform speed of 60km/hour for $3\frac{1}{2}$ hours when he stops 1 hour for tea. He then travels a further 100km at a uniform speed of 80km/hour to his destination. After 2 hours he returns home travelling at a uniform speed and arriving at 10 p.m. Draw a distant-time graph of his journey.

From your graph determine his speed on the return journey.

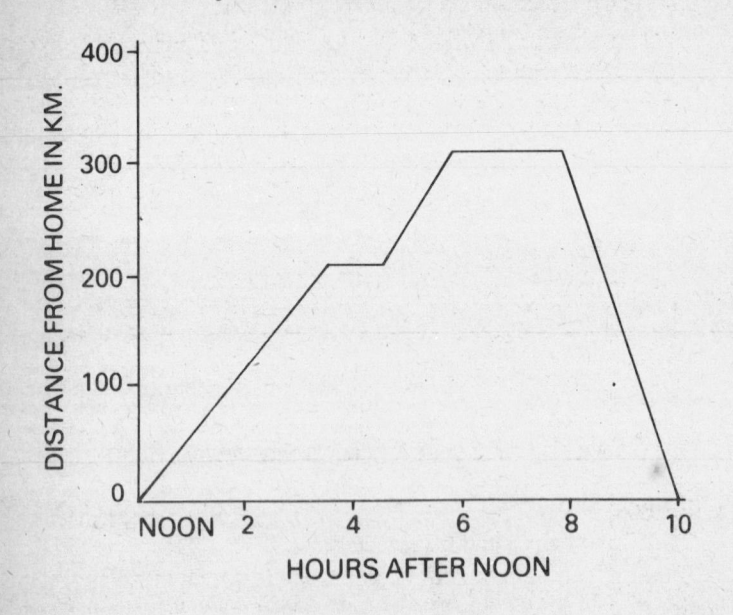

From graph—
    total distance travelled is 310km
    time to travel home is 2·25 hours
    speed on return journey $= \dfrac{310}{2\cdot 25}$ km/hr
                                $= \underline{137\cdot 8 \text{ km/hr (correct to 1 dec. pt.)}}$

PRACTICE QUESTIONS

1. A man starts from home at noon and travels at a uniform speed of 100km/hr. for 2 hours before stopping for half an hour. He then covers the next 150km of his journey in 1½ hours. After an hour's stop he returns home non-stop at a uniform speed of 100km/hr.

   Draw a distance-time graph of his journey. (Take 2cm to represent 1 hour and 2cm to represent 100km.)

   From your graph determine the total distance travelled and the time he reached home.

2. The diagram below shows an incomplete distance-time graph of a man who sets out from A at noon to keep an appointment at B 120km away at 3.40 p.m.
   (a) At what speed did he travel in the first 20 minutes?
   (b) Between what times did he stop?
   (c) If he travelled at a uniform speed for the remainder of his journey and reached B at 3.40 p.m. complete the graph.
   (d) What was his speed for the last part of his journey?
   (e) If he had travelled at a constant speed for the whole journey what would that speed have been?

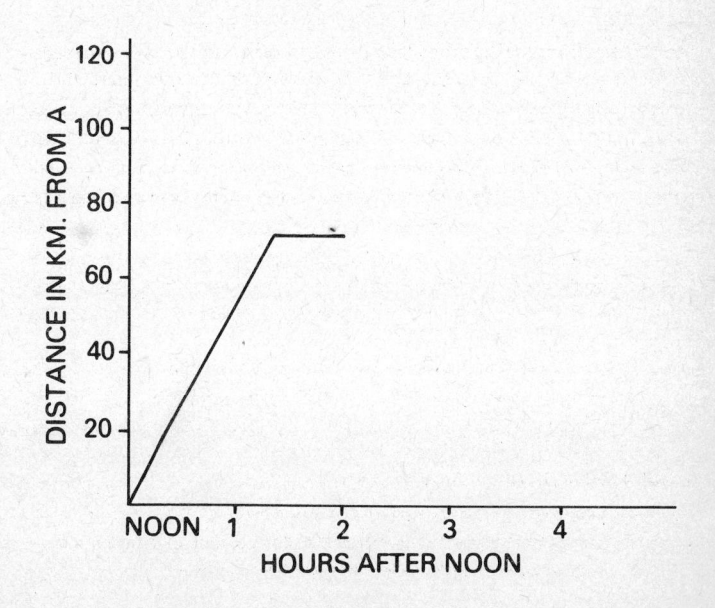

3. A man travels from A to B, a distance of 200km, by car. He leaves A at 9 a.m. and travels the first 120km at an average speed of 90km per hour. He then stops for 40 minutes at a service station before completing his journey at an average speed of 120km per hour. Draw a distant-time graph of his journey using 3cm to represent 1 hour and 1cm to represent 10km. Use your graph to determine when he left the service station and when he arrived at B.

A second man starts from B at 9.40 a.m. to travel to A. What are the average speeds between which he can travel in order for him to arrive at the service station while the first man is stopping there?

THE QUADRATIC FUNCTION

The **general quadratic function of x is** of the form $ax^2 + bx + c$, where a, b and c are constants. **The graph of $ax^2 + bx + c$ is a parabola.**

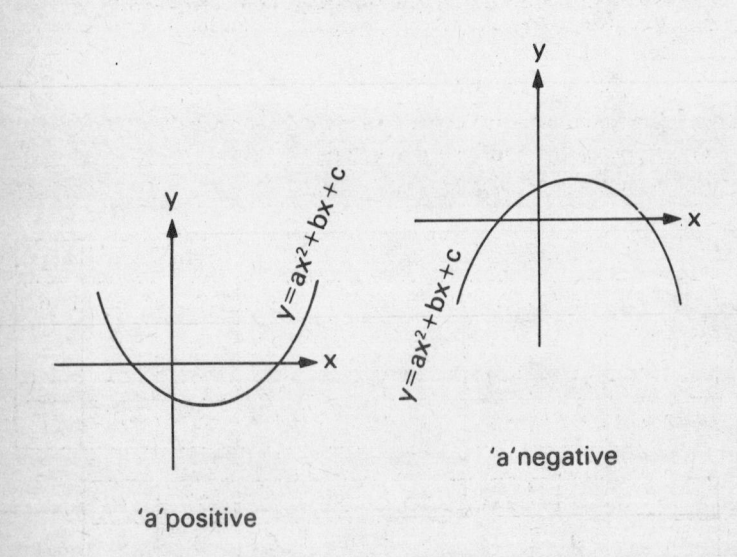

'a' positive

'a' negative

EXAMPLE

Copy and complete the table of values of the function $6 + 2x - x^2$.

x =	−2	−1½	−1	−½	0	½	1
6 =		6					
+ 2x =		−3					
− x² =		−2·25					
y = 6 + 2x − x² =		−0·75					

x =	1½	2	2½	3	3½	4
6 =		6				
+ 2x =		4				
− x² =		−4				
y = 6 + 2x − x² =		6				

Using 2cm to represent 1 unit on both axes draw the graph of $y = 6 + 2x - x^2$ from $x = -2$ to $x = 4$.

Use your graph to obtain:

(a) the solutions of the equation $6 + 2x - x^2 = 0$;
(b) the solutions of the equation $1·5 + 2x - x^2 = 0$;
(c) the values of x for which $6 + 2x - x^2 > 1$;
(d) the maximum value of $6 + 2x - x^2$.

x =	−2	−1½	−1	−½	0	½	1
6 =	6	6	6	6	6	6	6
+ 2x =	−4	−3	−2	−1	0	1	2
− x² =	−4	−2¼	−1	−¼	0	−¼	−1
y = 6 + 2x − x² =	−2	¾	3	4¾	6	6¾	7

x =	1½	2	2½	3	3½	4
6 =	6	6	6	6	6	6
+ 2x =	3	4	5	6	7	8
− x² =	−2¼	−4	−6¼	−9	−12¼	−16
y = 6 + 2x − x² =	6¾	6	4¾	3	¾	−2

$$y = 6 + 2x - x^2$$

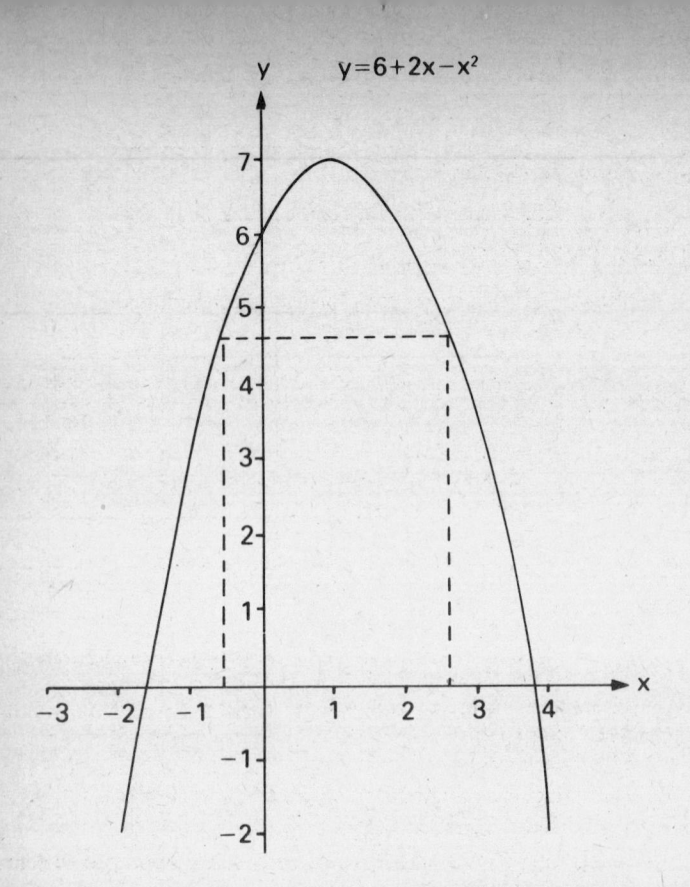

(a) From the graph of $y = 6 + 2x - x^2$ read off the values of x when
$\quad\quad y = 0$:
$\quad\quad y = 0$ when $x = 1\cdot 65$ and $3\cdot 65$
hence the solution of the equation $6 + 2x - x^2 = 0$ are
$\quad\quad \underline{x = -1\cdot 65 \text{ and } 3\cdot 65 \text{ (approx)}}$

(b) the eqn. $1\cdot 5 + 2x - x^2 = 0$ is the same as the eqn.
$\quad\quad 6 + 2x - x^2 = 4\cdot 5$ obtained by adding $4\cdot 5$
to both sides of the first equation.
From the graph $y = 4\cdot 5$ when $x = 0\cdot 6$ and $2\cdot 6$
hence the solutions of the eqn. $1\cdot 5 + 2x - x^2 = 0$ are
$\quad\quad \underline{x = -0\cdot 6 \text{ and } 2\cdot 6 \text{ (approx)}}$

(c) From the graph $y = 1$ when $x = -1 \cdot 45$ and $3 \cdot 45$,
hence $y > 1$ when x lies between $-1 \cdot 45$ and $3 \cdot 45$
i.e. $\underline{6 + 2x - x^2 > 1 \text{ when } -1 \cdot 45 < x < 3 \cdot 45.}$

(d) From the graph the max. y is 7
$\therefore$ $\underline{\text{the max. value of } 6 + 2x - x^2 \text{ is 7.}}$

PRACTICE QUESTIONS

1. Copy and complete the table of values of the function
$y = \frac{1}{2}(x^2 - 3x - 2)$.

x =	−3	−2	−1	0	1	2	3	4	5
$x^2 =$		4						16	
$-3x =$		6						−12	
$-2 =$		−2						−2	
$x^2 - 3x - 2 =$		8						2	
$y =$									

Using 1cm to represent 1 unit on both axes draw the graph of
$y = \frac{1}{2}(x^2 - 3x - 2)$ from $x = -3$ to $x = 5$,
plotting any extra points which are necessary to obtain an accurate graph.

Use your graph to:

(a) obtain the solutions to the equation $x^2 - 3x - 2 = 6$;
(b) find the minimum value of $\frac{1}{2}(x^2 - 3x - 2)$;
(c) obtain the value of the gradient of the tangent to the curve when $x = 2$.

2. Draw the graph of $y = x^2 + 2x = 8$ from $x = -4$ to $x = 6$ choosing suitable scales on each axis. Use your graph to:

(a) obtain solutions to the equations (i) $x^2 + 2x - 8 = 1$ (ii) $x^2 + 2x = 4$;
(b) the minimum value of $x^2 + 2x - 8$ and the value of x which gives this value;
(c) the range of values of x for which $x^2 + 2x < 8$.

GENERAL FUNCTIONS

The graph of a general function of x such as $\frac{3}{x + 6}$ or $x^3 + 3x^2 + \frac{1}{x}$, will give a smooth continuous curve for the range of values of x indicated in the given question. No new techniques are involved.

EXAMPLE

Draw the graph of $\frac{30}{x + 6}$ from $x = -3.5$ to $x = 5.5$ by first copying and completing the following table.

Let 2cm represent 1 unit on the x axis and 1cm represent 1 unit on the y axis.

With the same scales and axes draw the graph of $6 - x$.

(a) Show that the values of x at the intersections of the graphs give solutions of the equation,

$$x^2 = 6$$

and find the two solutions from your graphs.

(b) Use your graphs to find a range of values of x for which,

$$\frac{30}{x + 6} - 2 \leqslant 6 - x$$

	−3·5	−3	−2	−1	0	1	2	3	4	5	5·5
x + 6 =		3		5				9			
$\frac{30}{x + 6} =$				6				3·33			

The completed table is:

x =	−3·5	−3	−2	−1	0	1	2	3	4	5	5·5
x + 6 =	2·5	3	4	5	6	7	8	9	10	11	11·5
$\frac{30}{x + 6} =$	12	10	7·5	6	5	4·29	3·75	3·33	3	2·72	2·61

$$y = 6 - x$$

x =	−2	0	2
y =	8	6	4

(a) At points of intersection

$$\frac{30}{x + 6} = 6 - x$$

i.e. $30 = (6 - x)(6 + x)$

$30 = 36 - x^2$

$\underline{x^2 = 6}$

The x-coords. of the points of intersection are
Hence the roots of $x^2 = 6$ are $\underline{x = \pm 2\cdot 45.}$

$$\frac{30}{x + 6} - 2 \leqslant 6 - x$$

$$\therefore \frac{30}{x + 6} \leqslant 8 - x.$$

Now $y = 8 - x$ is parallel to $y = 6 - x$

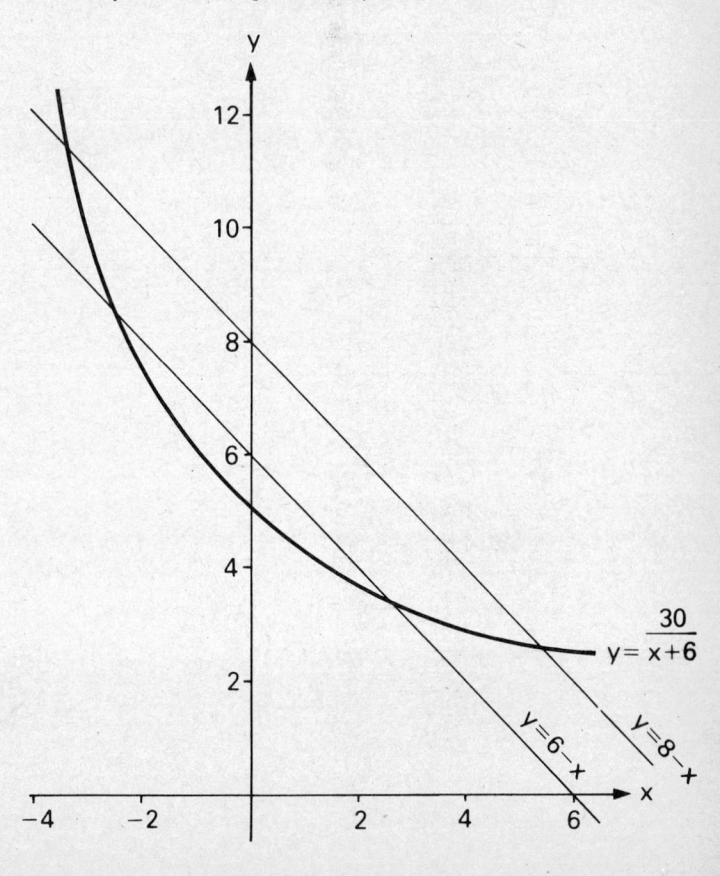

Through (0,8) draw line parallel to $y = 6 - x$. This line is the line $y = 8 - x$.

At points of intersection of $y = \dfrac{30}{x+6}$ and $y = 8 - x$ the x-coordinates are $x = +5\cdot32$ and $-3\cdot36$

$\therefore \dfrac{30}{x+6} - 2 \leqslant 6 - x$ when $\underline{-3\cdot36 \leqslant x \leqslant 5\cdot36}$.

PRACTICE QUESTIONS

1. The coordinates of A are $(5, -13)$ and of B are $(10, 12)$. Calculate: (a) the length of AB to 3 s.f.; (b) the gradient of AB; (c) the equations of AB; (d) the equation of the line through C $(-1, -4)$ parallel to AB.

2. Copy and complete the table of values of the function $x^2 - 4x + 2$.

x =	−1	−½	0	½	1	1½
x^2 =	1					2¼
−4x =	4					−6
+2 =	2					2
$x^2 - 4x + 2$ =	7					−1¾

x =	2	2½	3	3½	4	5
x^2 =					16	
−4x =					−16	
+2 =			2		2	
$x^2 - 4x + 2$ =					2	

Draw the graph of $y = x^2 - 4x + 2$ taking 2cm to represent 1 unit on both axes.

Use your graph to obtain:

(a) the solution of the equation $x^2 - 4x + 2 = 0$;

(b) the solutions of the equation $x^2 - 4x - 1 = 0$;

(c) the values of x for which $x^2 - 4x + 2 < 4$;

(d) the values of x for which $x^2 - 4x + 2 \geqslant 5$;
(e) the minimum value of $x^2 - 4x + 2$.

3. Copy and complete the following table when
$$y = \frac{12}{x} + x$$

x =	1	2	3	4	5	6	7	8
$\frac{12}{x} =$		6			2·4			
y =		8			7·4			

Draw the graph of $y = \frac{12}{x} + x$ from $x = 1$ to $x = 8$.

From your graph find the minimum value of $\frac{12}{x} + x$.

With the same scales and axes draw the graph of $y = x(8 - x)$. from $x = 0$ to $x = 8$, and hence find two solutions to the equation:
$$\frac{12}{x} + x = x(8 - x)$$

4. A pump empties oil from a storage tank so that W tonnes are emptied in t hours where:
$$W = t^2 (32 - t).$$

Plot a graph of W against t from $t = 0$ to $t = 8$. Take 2cm to represent 1 hour and 1cm to represent 100 tonnes of oil.

If a full tank holds 1500 tonnes of oil, find from your graph

(a) how long the pump takes to empty a full tank.
(b) how long the pump takes to deliver 400 tonnes from a full tank.

5. Draw on the same sheet of graph paper, with the same axes, the graphs of $y = \frac{12}{x + 1}$ and $y = 10 + x - x^2$, for values of x from 0 to 4 inclusive at ½ unit intervals.

State why your graphs will give solutions to the equation $x^3 - 11x + 2 = 0$ and find two such solutions.

TRIGONOMETRY
DEFINITIONS

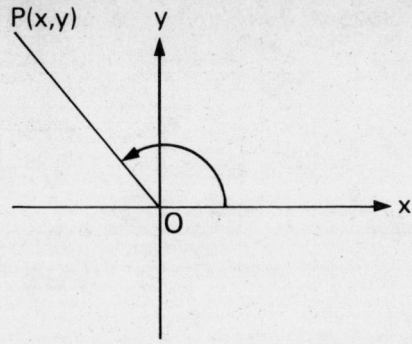

Let OP be an anticlockwise rotating radius, starting with OP on Ox in the x−y plane. When P reaches a position with coordinates (X, Y) let $\angle xOP = \theta$. Then:

$$\sin \theta = \frac{Y}{OP} \qquad \cos \theta = \frac{X}{OP} \qquad \tan \theta = \frac{Y}{X}.$$

EXAMPLES

1.

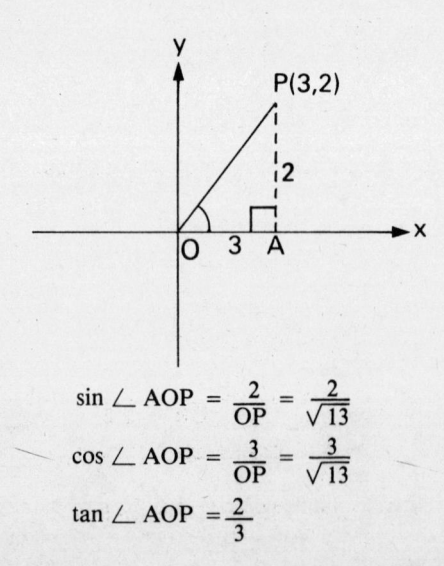

$$\sin \angle AOP = \frac{2}{OP} = \frac{2}{\sqrt{13}}$$

$$\cos \angle AOP = \frac{3}{OP} = \frac{3}{\sqrt{13}}$$

$$\tan \angle AOP = \frac{2}{3}$$

2.

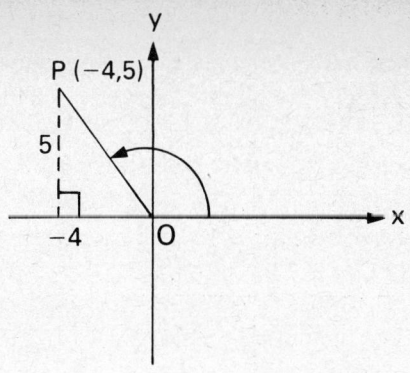

$$\sin \angle xOP = \frac{5}{OP} = \frac{5}{\sqrt{41}}$$

$$\cos \angle xOP = \frac{-4}{OP} = -\frac{4}{\sqrt{41}}$$

$$\tan \angle xOP = \frac{5}{-4} = -1\cdot 25$$

3.

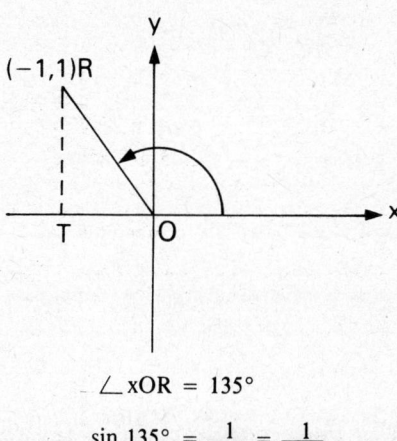

$$\angle xOR = 135°$$

$$\sin 135° = \frac{1}{OR} = \frac{1}{\sqrt{2}}$$

$$\cos 135° = \frac{-1}{\sqrt{2}}$$

$$\tan 135° = \frac{-1}{1} = -1$$

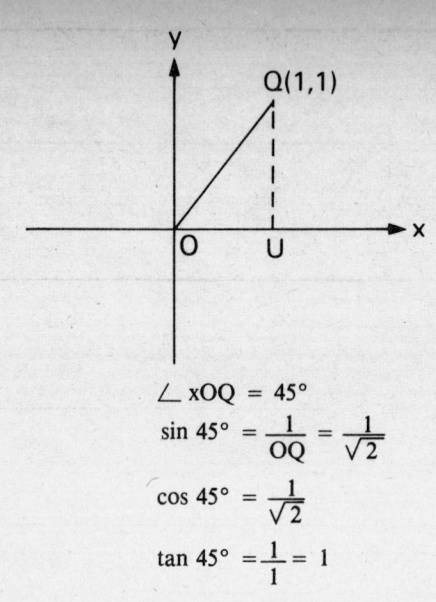

$\angle xOQ = 45°$

$\sin 45° = \dfrac{1}{OQ} = \dfrac{1}{\sqrt{2}}$

$\cos 45° = \dfrac{1}{\sqrt{2}}$

$\tan 45° = \dfrac{1}{1} = 1$

The third example illustrates the following results which arise from the original definitions:

(a) The sine of an obtuse angle equals the sine of its supplement;
(b) The cosine of an obtuse angle equals minus the cosine of its supplement;
(c) The tangent of an obtuse angle equals minus the tangent of its supplement.

4.

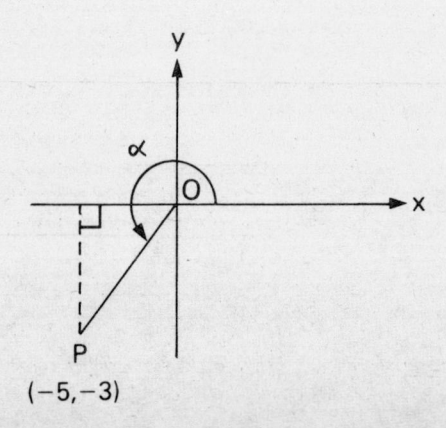

The angle is now the reflex angle xOP = α say

$$\sin \alpha = \frac{-3}{OP} = -\frac{3}{\sqrt{34}}$$

$$\cos \alpha = \frac{-5}{OP} = -\frac{5}{\sqrt{34}}$$

$$\tan \alpha = \frac{-3}{-5} = \frac{3}{5}$$

5. Find the sine, cosine and tangent of the following angles, using your trigonometric tables:
   (a) 48° 53′,   (b) 125° 32′,   (c) 147° 14′,   (d) 200°.

   (a) sin 48° 53′ = 0·7534,
       cos 48° 53′ = 0·6576,
       tan 48° 53′ = 1·1456.

   (b) 180° − 125° 32′ = 54° 28′, therefore:
       sin 125° 32′ = sin 54° 28′ = 0·8138,
       cos 125° 32′ = − cos 54° 28′ = − 0·5812,
       tan 125° 32′ = − tan 54° 28′ = − 1·4002.

   (c) 180° − 147° 14′ = 32° 46′, therefore:
       sin 147° 14′ = sin 32° 46′ = 0·5413,
       cos 147° 14′ = − cos 32° 46′ = − 0·8409,
       tan 147° 14′ = − tan 32° 46′ = − 0·6437.

   (d) 200° − 180° = 20°, therefore:
       sin 200° = − sin 20° = − 0·3420,
       cos 200° = − cos 20° = − 0·9397,
       tan 200° = tan 20° = 0·3640.

   N.B. 1. Sines and cosines are always numerically less than 1. Tangents of angles less than 45° are less than 1. Tangents of angles greater than 45° are greater than 1.

   2. The differences in the cosines are subtracted as you add the corresponding minutes of arc.

SPECIAL ANGLES 30°, 60°, 45°

The trigonometric functions of these angles may be written down without using tables. Remember the following two triangles.

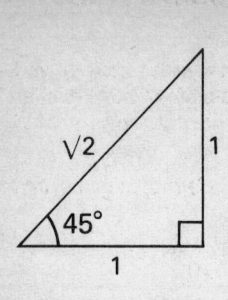

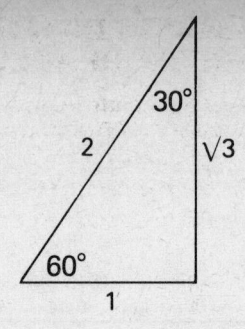

$$\sin 45° = \frac{1}{\sqrt{2}}$$
$$\cos 45° = \frac{1}{\sqrt{2}}$$
$$\tan 45° = 1$$

$$\sin 60° = \frac{\sqrt{3}}{2} = \cos 30°$$
$$\cos 60° = \frac{1}{2} = \sin 30°$$
$$\tan 60° = \sqrt{3}$$
$$\tan 30° = \frac{1}{\sqrt{3}}$$

PRACTICE QUESTIONS

1. Find the sine, cosine and tangent of:
   (a) 35° 17′,
   (b) 129° 33′,
   (c) 197° 54′,
   (d) 320°.

2. Write down the values of:
   (i) log sin 23° 14′,
   (ii) log tan 67° 18′,
   (iii) log sin 137° 18′,
   (iv) log cos 8° 36′.

3. Evaluate:
   (i) 3 − 4 cos 150°,
   (ii) $\dfrac{3}{\sin 30°}$,
   (iii) $\dfrac{\tan 40°}{\tan 135°}$,
   (iv) $\cos^2 157°$.

EXAMPLES INVOLVING SINE, COSINE AND TANGENT OF ANGLES

1. O is the centre of a circle. From a point A which is 12cm from O, a tangent AT is drawn to the circle, touching the circle at T. $\angle$ OAT = 36°. Calculate, to three significant figures:
   (a) the radius of the circle;
   (b) the length of the chord through T perpendicular to OA.

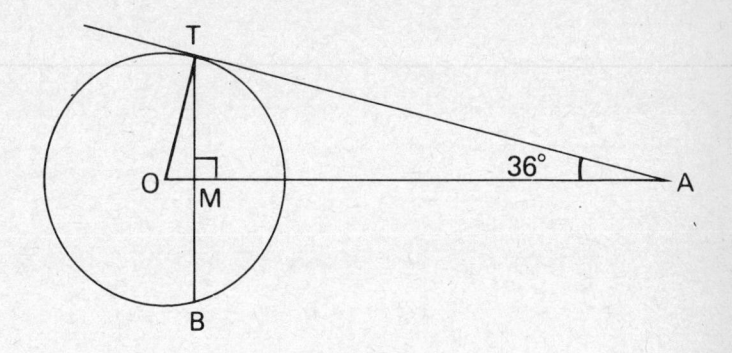

(a) Since AT is a tangent at T, $\angle$ OTA = 90°.

   in $\triangle$ OTA $\dfrac{OT}{OA}$ = sin 36°

   OT = OA sin 36°

   = 12 × 0·5878
   = 7·0536

   ∴ **radius of the circle is 7·05cm to 3 s.f.**

   $\angle$ TOA = 90° − 36° = 54°

(b) In rt. $\angle$ d $\triangle$ OTM

   $\dfrac{TM}{OT}$ = sin 54°

   TM = 7·0536 × sin 54°

   TM = 5·707
   TB = 2TM = 11·414
   ∴ **TB is 11·4cm to 3 s.f.**

No.	log
7·0536	0·8484
sin 54	$\bar{1}$·9080
TM	0·7564

2. ABCD is a trapezium with AB parallel to DC, AB = AD = BC and $\angle$ ADC = $\angle$ BCD = 58° 30'. The perpendicular distance between AB and DC is 6·75cm.

Calculate:

(a) the lengths of AB and CD;

(b) the area of the trapezium.

Give answers to 3 s.f.

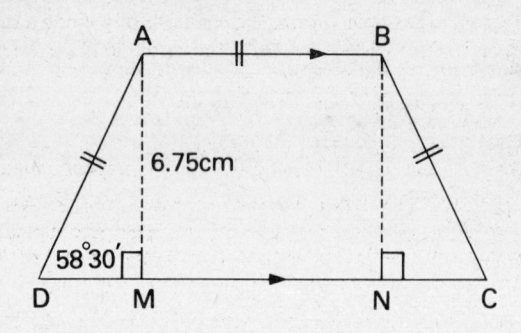

(a) Draw AM and BN perpendicular to DC.

In $\triangle$ ADM

$$\frac{6 \cdot 75}{AD} = \sin 58° 30'$$

$$AD = \frac{6 \cdot 75}{\sin 58° 30'}$$

$$= 7 \cdot 916$$

AD = 7·92cm to 3 s.f.

∴ **AB = 7·92cm to 3 s.f.**

No.	log
6·75	0·8293
sin 58° 30'	$\overline{1}$·9308
	0·8985

$\angle$ DAM = 90° − 58° 30' = 31° 30'

$$\frac{DM}{AM} = \tan 31° 30'$$

DM = 6·75 tan 31° 30'

= 4·136

DM = NC

DC = DM + MN + NC and MN = AB

∴ DC = 4·136 + 7·916 + 4·136

= 16·188

DC = 16·19cm to 3 s.f.

	logs
	0·8293
	$\overline{1}$·7873
	0·6166

Area trapezium ABCD = $\frac{1}{2}$ (7·916 + 16·188) × 6·75cm^2
= 81·351
∴ Area ABCD = 81·35cm^2 to 3 s.f.

PRACTICE QUESTIONS

N.B. Give answers to three significant figures.

1. From a point P 15cm from the centre O of a circle a tangent PT is drawn to the circle, touching the circle at T. ∠ TOP = 52°. Calculate:
   (a) the radius of the circle;
   (b) the length PT;
   (c) the length of the chord through T perpendicular to OP.

2. ABCD is a trapezium with AB parallel to DC, AB = 3·6cm, ∠ ADC = 53° and ∠ BCD = 66°. The perpendicular distance between AB and DC is 11cm. Calculate the lengths of AD, BC and CD, and the area of the trapezium.

3. PQRS is a rhombus with sides 7·3cm long. ∠ PQR is 55°. Calculate the lengths of the diagonals of PQRS, and the area of PQRS.

4. A man walks from A to B, a distance of 4·5km, on a bearing of 065°. At B he changes direction to a bearing of 163° and walks a further 12km to C. How far is C East and South of A?

THE SINE RULE AND COSINE RULE

When the given diagram does not contain right-angled triangles the sine and/or cosine rules can be used.

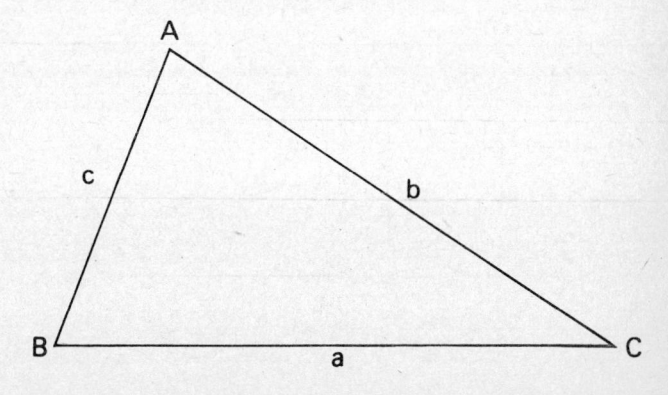

The Sine Rule
$$\frac{a}{\sin A} = \frac{b}{\sin B} = \frac{c}{\sin C}$$

This rule is applied when we are given two angles and a side of the triangle.

It is also applied when we are given one angle and the side opposite that angle, and another side in order to calculate the angle opposite this second side. Care must be taken in this case to use the data in the question to determine whether the angle calculated is acute or obtuse.

The Cosine Rule
$$a^2 = b^2 + c^2 - 2bc \cos A$$
$$b^2 = c^2 + a^2 - 2ca \cos B$$
$$c^2 = a^2 + b^2 - 2ab \cos C$$

This rule is applied when we are given

(a) two sides and the angle included between these sides;

(b) the three sides.

When the three sides are given the cosine rule equations are rearranged:

$$a^2 = b^2 + c^2 - 2bc \cos A \text{ becoming } \cos A = \frac{b^2 + c^2 - a^2}{2bc}, \text{ etc.}$$

EXAMPLES

1. Two fixed marking buoys, A and B, are 2·3km apart. A is due North of B. From a ship, C, the buoy A is a bearing of 286° and

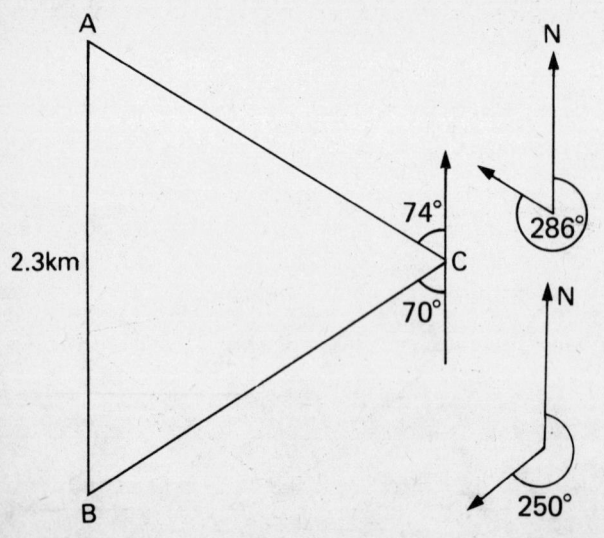

the buoy B is on a bearing of 250°. Calculate the distance of the ship from buoy A, in km to 3 s.f.

$$360° - 286° = 74° \qquad 250° - 180° = 70°$$

To find AC:

In $\triangle$ ABC, $\angle$ A = 74°, $\angle$ B = 70° (Alt. $\angle$ s | |lines)

$$\therefore \angle C = 36°$$

By sine rule $\dfrac{b}{\sin B} = \dfrac{c}{\sin C}$

$$\dfrac{AC}{\sin 70°} = \dfrac{2 \cdot 3}{\sin 36°}$$

$$AC = \dfrac{2 \cdot 3 \sin 70°}{\sin 36°}$$

$$= 3 \cdot 677$$

logs
0·3617
$\bar{1}$·9730
0·3347
$\bar{1}$·7692
0·5655

∴ Ship is 3·68km to 3 s.f.

2. In the quadrilateral ABCD, AB = 9cm, BC = 8cm, CD = 7cm, and AD = 10cm. $\angle$ ABC = 135°12'. Calculate:

(a) AC;

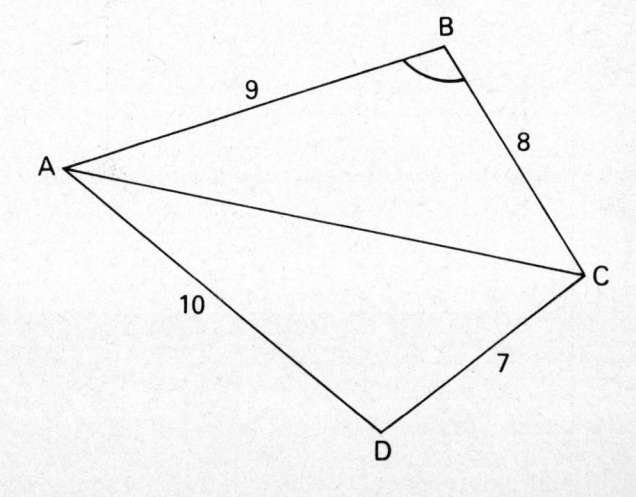

(b) $\angle$ ADC.

(a) In ABC, by cosine rule, $b^2 = c^2 + a^2 - 2ca \cos B$

$b^2 = 9^2 + 8^2 - 2 \times 9 \times 8 \times \cos 135° 12'$
$= 81 + 64 + 2 \times 9 \times 8 \cos 44° 48'$
$= 81 + 64 + 144 \cos 44° 48'$
$= 81 + 64 + 102 \cdot 2$
$b^2 = 247 \cdot 2$
$\therefore b = \sqrt{247 \cdot 2}$
$= 15 \cdot 73$

$\therefore \underline{AC = 15 \cdot 7 \text{cm to 3 s.f.}}$

No.	logs
144	2·1584
cos 44° 48'	$\bar{1}$·8510
	2·0094

N.B. 1. $\cos 135° 12' = - \cos 44° 48'$

2. $2 \times 9 \times 8 \cos 44° 48'$ is evaluated, then 81 and 64 added to the result.

(b) In △ ACD, by cosine rule, $\cos \angle D = \dfrac{a^2 + c^2 - d^2}{2ac}$,

$\cos \angle D = \dfrac{7^2 + 10^2 - 247 \cdot 2}{2 \times 7 \times 10}$

$= \dfrac{49 + 100 - 247 \cdot 2}{140}$

$= \dfrac{149 - 247 \cdot 2}{140}$

$\cos \angle D = - \dfrac{98 \cdot 2}{140}$

No.	logs
98·2	1·9921
140	2·1461
cos 32° 13'	$\bar{1}$·8460

$\therefore \angle D = 180° - 32° 13'$
$= 47° 47'$

i.e. $\underline{\angle ADC = 47° 47'}$

PRACTICE QUESTIONS

1. Two fixed marking buoys, P and Q, are 4·1km apart. P is due North of Q. From a ship, R, the buoy P is on a bearing of 279° and the buoy Q is on a bearing of 241° 30'. Calculate the distance of the ship from buoy Q, in km to 3 s.f.

2. In the quadrilateral PQRS, $\angle SPQ = 140°$, PQ = 11cm, QR = 9cm, RS = 12cm and PS = 8cm.
   Calculate: (a) QS; (b) $\angle QRS$.

3. Observer B is 10km due North of observer A. A ship is sighted due West of B (bearing 270°) and on a bearing of 310° from A. The

ship sails at a steady speed, on a constant course for 1 hour when it is due West of A and on a bearing of 240° from B. Find the speed and course of the ship.

4. An obtuse angled triangle ABC is such that AC = 40mm, AB = 60mm and ∠ BAC = 30°. D is the foot of the perpendicular from B to AC produced. Calculate: (a) BC; (b) ∠ BCA; (c) BD; (d) CD.

5. ABCD is a cyclic quadrilateral. AD = 18cm, DC = 26cm and AC = 21cm. AB = BC. Calculate: (a) ∠ ADC; (b) the length of AB; (c) the area of the quadrilateral ABCD.

VARIATION

DIRECT VARIATION

One variable y is said to "vary directly as", or to "vary as", or "to be proportional to" another variable x if:

$$\frac{y_1}{x_1} = \frac{y_2}{x_2} \,(= k)$$

where (x_1, y_1) are one pair of values of x and y and (x_2, y_2) any other pairs of values of x and y. k is the constant value of $\frac{y}{x}$ for all pairs of values of x and y.

In symbols, $y \propto x$, which as an equation is

$$y = kx.$$

If all pairs of values of two variables x and y are such that $y = kx^n$ where n,k are constants, we say that y varies directly as x^n or y varies as x^n, or y is proportional to x^n.

N.B. When $y \propto x$, as x increases, y increases.

When $y \propto x^n$ as x^n increases y increases.

INVERSE VARIATION

One variable y is said to "vary inversely as x", or "y is proportional to $\frac{1}{x}$", if $x_1 y_1 = x_2 y_2 \,(= k)$ where (x_1, y_1) are one pair of values of x and y and (x_2, y_2) any other pair of values of x and y. k is the constant value of xy for all pairs of values of x and y.

In symbols $y \propto \frac{1}{x}$, which as an equation is

$$xy = k.$$

If all pairs of values of two variables x and y are such that $y = \dfrac{k}{x^n}$ where n, k are constants, we say that y varies inversely as x^n, or y is proportional to $\dfrac{1}{x^n}$.

N.B. When $y \propto \dfrac{1}{x}$, as x increases y decreases.

When $y \propto \dfrac{1}{x^n}$ as x^n increases y decreases.

EXAMPLES

1. y varies as the square of x, and y = 48 when x = 4. Calculate:
   (a) the value of y when x = −5;
   (b) the values of x when y = 12.

   Draw a sketch graph of y in terms of x.

   $$y \propto x^2$$
   $$y = kx^2 \text{ where k is a constant}$$
   $$y = 48 \text{ when } x = 4, \text{ given}$$
   $$48 = k \times 16$$
   $$k = 3$$
   $$\therefore y = 3x^2$$

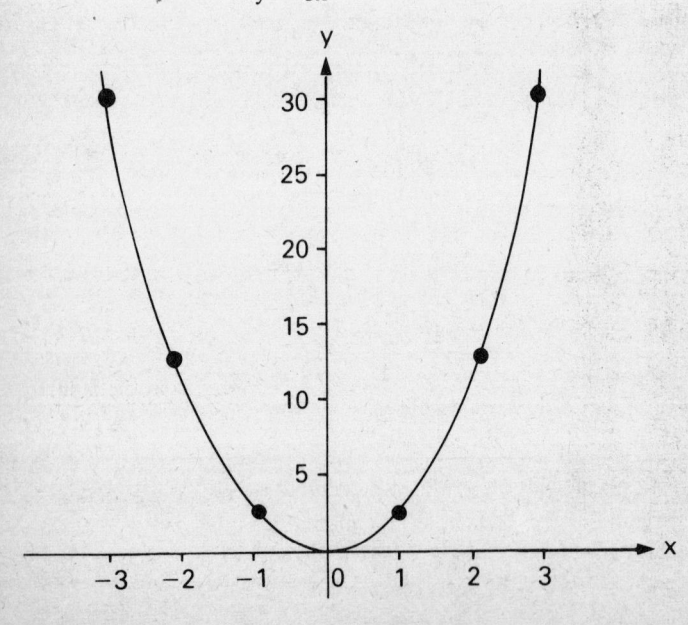

when $x = -5$, $\underline{y = 3 \times 25 = 75}$
when $y = 12$, $12 = 3x^2$
$$4 = x^2$$
$$\underline{x = \pm 2}.$$

$x =$	0	±1	±2	±3	....
$y =$	0	3	12	27	....

2. The intensity of illumination given by an electric light bulb varies inversely as the square of the distance of the point illuminated from the bulb. A point is illuminated at a distance of 4m from the bulb. Where must a second point be placed in order to receive twice the intensity of illumination of the first?

Let the intensity of illumination be I at a distance of d m from the lamp, then

$$I \propto \frac{1}{d^2}$$

or $I = \frac{k}{d^2}$ where k is a constant.

when $d = 4m$: $I_1 = \frac{k}{16}$

when $d = xm$: $I_2 = \frac{k}{x^2}$

when $I_2 = 2I_1$

$$\frac{k}{x^2} = 2\frac{k}{16}$$

i.e. $x^2 = 8$

$$x = 2\sqrt{2}$$

the second point must be placed $2\sqrt{2}$m from the bulb.

PRACTICE QUESTIONS

1. y varies (directly) as x, and $y = 5$ when $x = 3$. Calculate:
   (a) the value of y when $x = 2$;
   (b) the value of y when $x = -3$;
   (c) the value of x when $y = 12$.

Draw a graph to show the connection between y and x from x = − 4 to x = 8.

2. If y is inversely proportional to x^3 and $y = \frac{1}{4}$ when x = 2, find (a) the value of y when x = − 3 and (b) the value of x when $y = \frac{1}{36}$.

3. If a stone is dropped from a tower, the time taken to reach the ground is directly proportional to the square root of the height from which it is dropped. If the time taken to fall from a tower 62·5m high is 2·5 seconds, how long would it take to fall from a tower 160m high?

4. The intensity of illumination given by a light source varies inversely as the square of the distance of the point illuminated from the source. A point is illuminated at a distance of 3m from the source. Where must the point be moved to in order to receive only one quarter of the original intensity of illumination?

5. The horse-power produced by a car engine is proportional to the cube of the speed which the car attains. At speed s the horse-power produced is H. Calculate (a) the increase in horse-power needed to double the speed and (b) the speed attained when the horse-power is halved.

6. Z varies as the product of x and y. If z = − 8 when x = 3 and y = 4, find (a) z when x = − 6 and y = 10 and (b) x when z = 12 and y = 6.

7. A rectangle with variable length and breadth xcm and ycm respectively has a constant area of $64cm^2$. Plot y against x from $x = \frac{1}{2}$ to x = 30. What will be the dimensions of the rectangle when its perimeter is a minimum?

PLANE GEOMETRY

SUMMARY OF MAIN THEOREMS

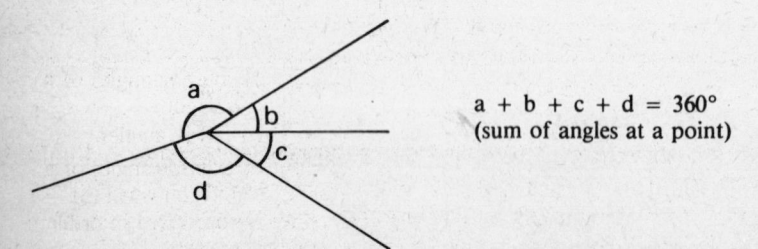

$a + b + c + d = 360°$
(sum of angles at a point)

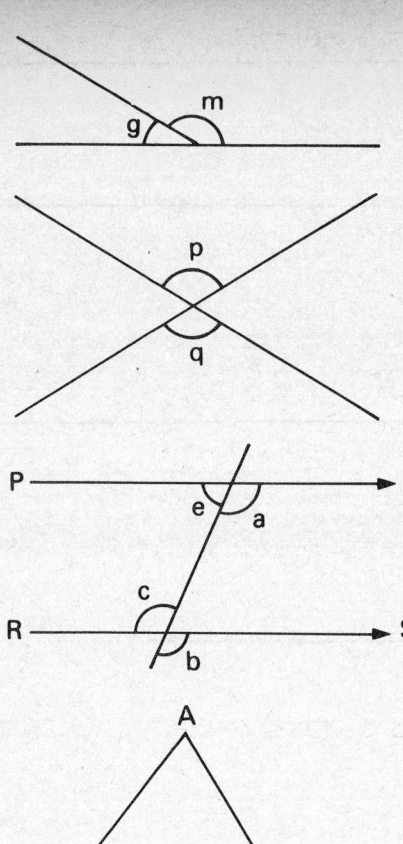

$g + m = 180°$ (adjacent angles on straight line)

$p = q$ (vertically opposite angles)

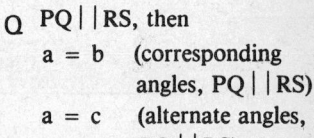

PQ∥RS, then
$a = b$ (corresponding angles, PQ∥RS)
$a = c$ (alternate angles, PQ∥RS)
$c + e = 180°$ (interior angles, PQ∥RS)

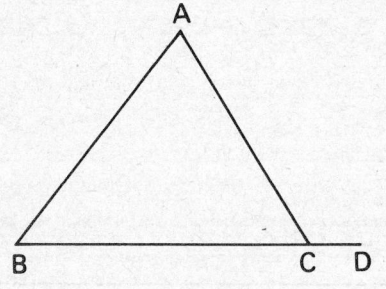

∠ACD = ∠A + ∠B (exterior angle of triangle)

∠A + ∠B + ∠ACB = 180°
(angle sum of triangle)

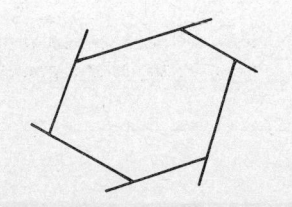

Sum of interior angles of a convex polygon
= (2n − 4) rt. angles

Sum of exterior angles of a convex polygon when the sides are produced in order
= 4 rt. angles.

Tests for congruence of two triangles are
1. (S S S)   2. (S A S)   3. (A A S) or (A S A)
In addition when the two triangles are right angled, we may also use (R H S)

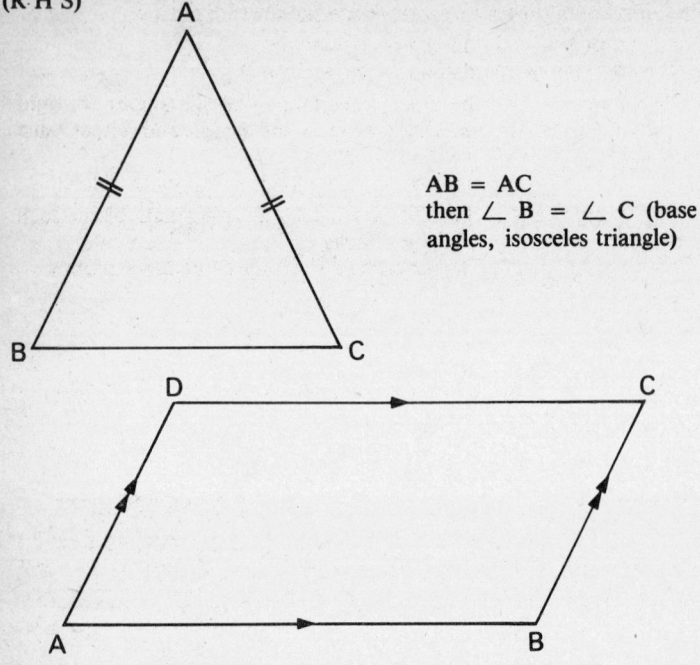

AB = AC
then ∠ B = ∠ C (base angles, isosceles triangle)

ABCD is a parallelogram,
then AB = CD and AD = BC (opposite sides parallelogram)
      ∠ A = ∠ C and ∠ D = ∠ B (opposite angles parallelogram)

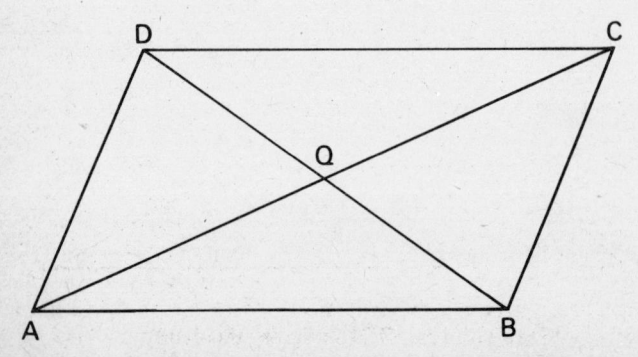

ABCD is a parallelogram
then AQ = QC and DQ = QB (intersecting diagonals, parallelogram)
Each diagonal bisects the area of the parallelogram.

The following additional properties are possessed by:

(a) **a rectangle** — All the angles right angles
  The diagonals are equal

(b) **a square** — All the sides are equal and all the angles are right angles, the diagonals are equal and bisect each other at right angles.
  A diagonal makes an angle of 45° with a side.

(c) **a rhombus** — All the sides are equal, the diagonals bisect each other at right angles.
  The diagonals bisect the angles of the rhombus.

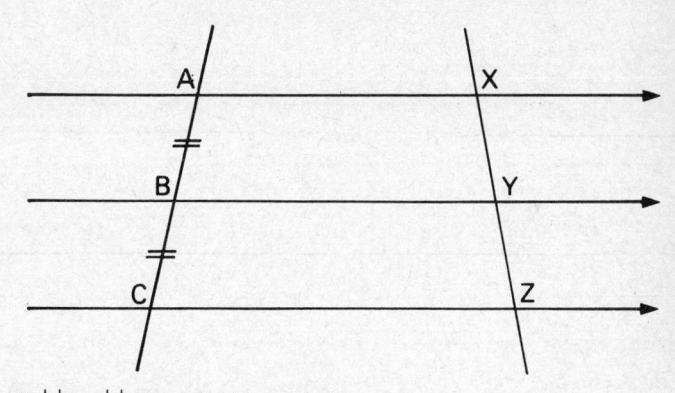

AX||BY||CZ and AB = BC
then XY = YZ (intercept theorem)

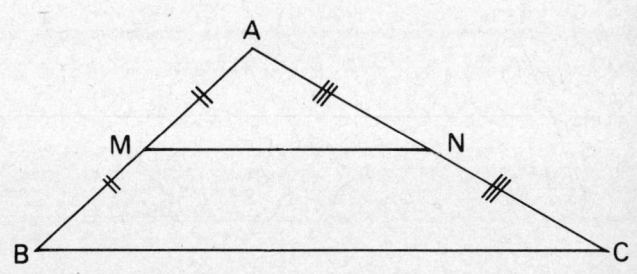

AM = BM and AN = CN
then MN||BC and MN = ½BC (mid-point theorem)

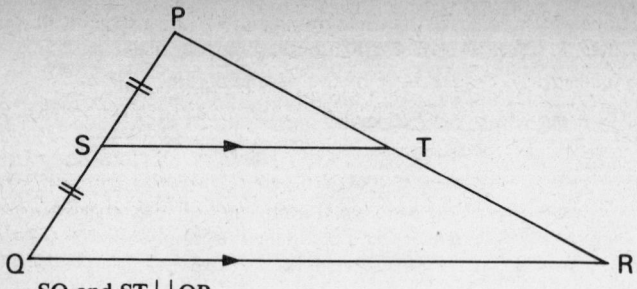

PS = SQ and ST||QR
then PT = RT (intercept theorem)

Two triangles are similar if:
   the triangles are equiangular,
OR the three sides of the one are proportional to the three sides of the other,
OR one angle of the one triangle is equal to an angle of the other and the sides about these equal angles are proportional.

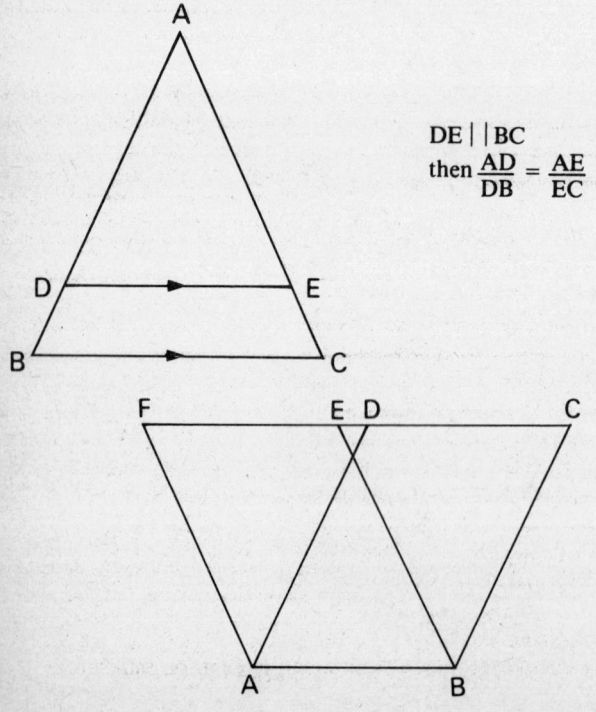

DE||BC
then $\dfrac{AD}{DB} = \dfrac{AE}{EC}$

If ABCD and ABEF are parallelograms and FEDC a straight line then
Area ABCD = Area ABEF (same base, same parallels).

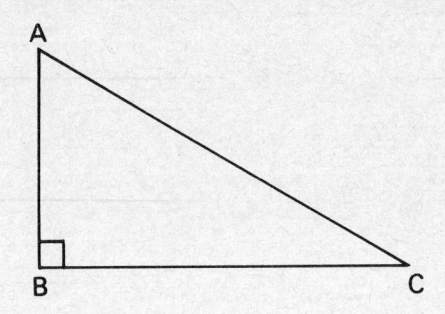

∠ ABC = 1 right angle
then $AB^2 + BC^2 = AC^2$ (Pythagoras)
and in trig. form $\sin^2 C + \cos^2 C = 1$.

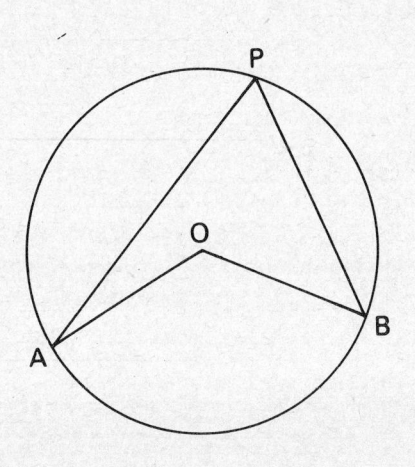

O is centre of the circle
∠ AOB = 2 ∠ APB (angles at centre and circum. on same arc)

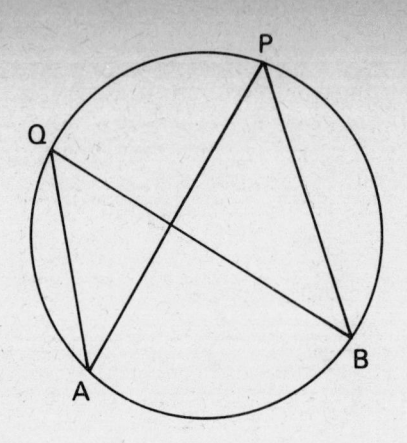

∠ AQB = ∠ APB (angles in same segment)
∠ QAP = ∠ QBP (angles in same segment)

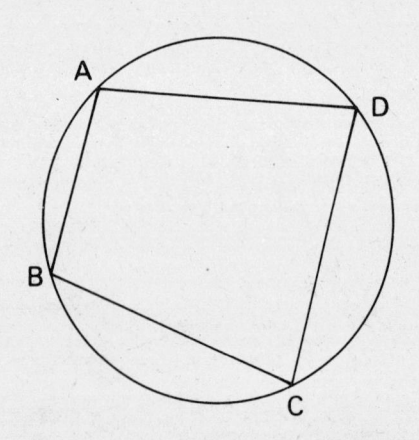

∠ A + ∠ C = 180° (opp. angles cyclic quad)
∠ B + ∠ D = 180°

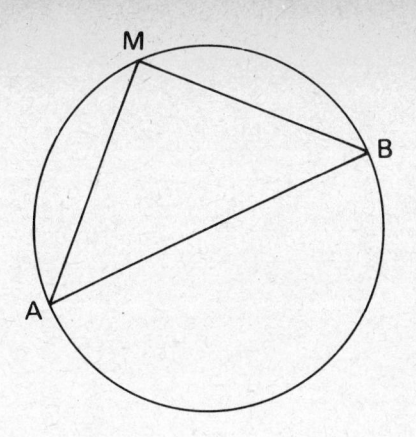

AB is a diameter
then ∠M = 90° (∠ in semi-circle)

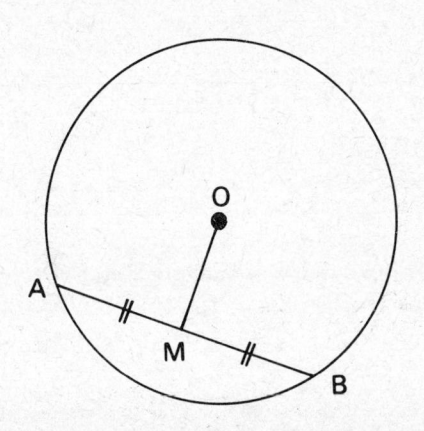

O centre of circle
M centre of chord AB
then OM is perpendicular to AB.

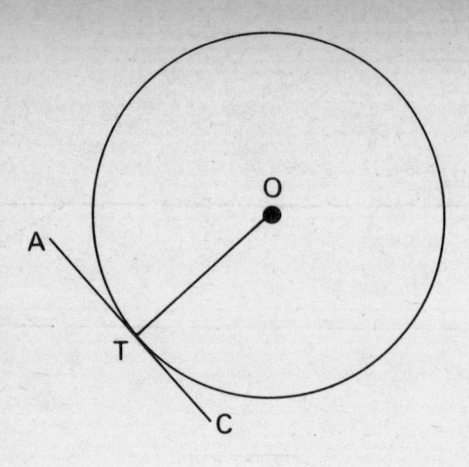

ATC is a tangent with point of contact at T. O centre of circle then OT is perpendicular to ATC (tangent and radius at point of contact).

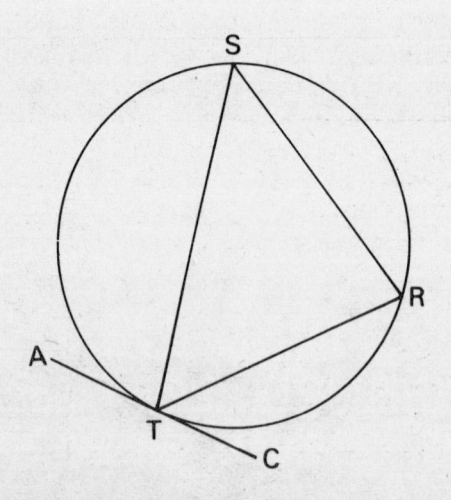

ATC is a tangent with point of contact at T.
Then $\angle$ CTR = $\angle$ TSR (alternate segment)
and $\angle$ ATS = $\angle$ TRS (alternate segment)

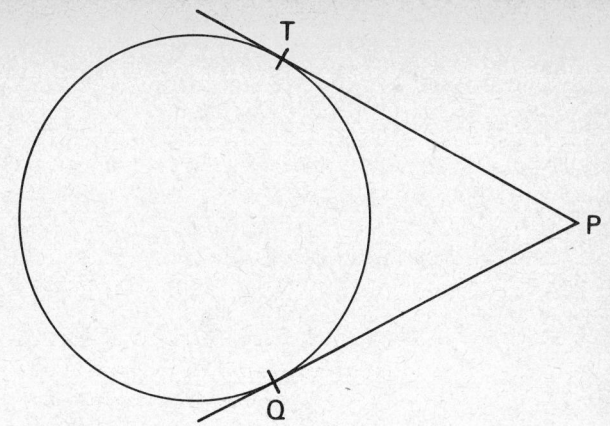

PT and PQ touch circle at T and Q respectively
then PT = PQ (tangents from external point)

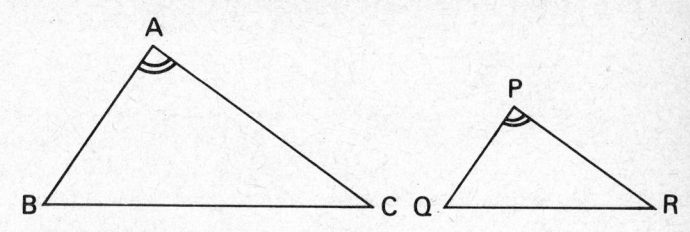

Δ ABC is similar to Δ PQR
then $\frac{\text{Area } \Delta \text{ ABC}}{\text{Area } \Delta \text{ PQR}} = \frac{BC^2}{QR^2}$

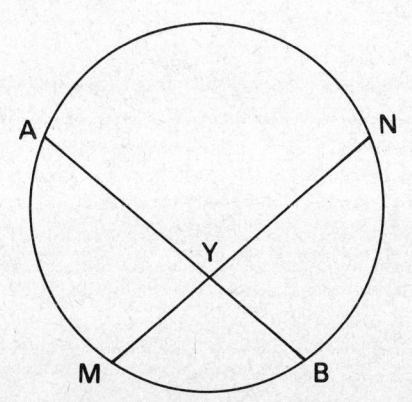

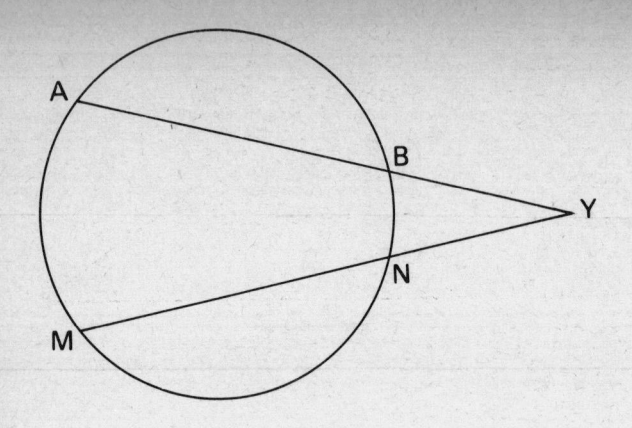

In both diagrams AY. YB = MY. YN (intersecting chords, rectangle property of circle)

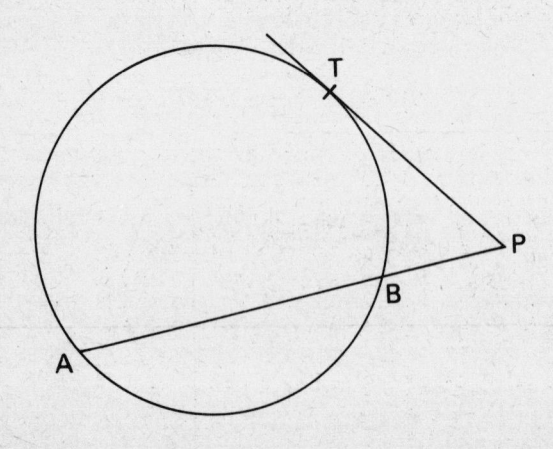

TP is tangent to the circle at T.
then TP^2 = PA. PB (tangent and secant, rectangle property of circle)

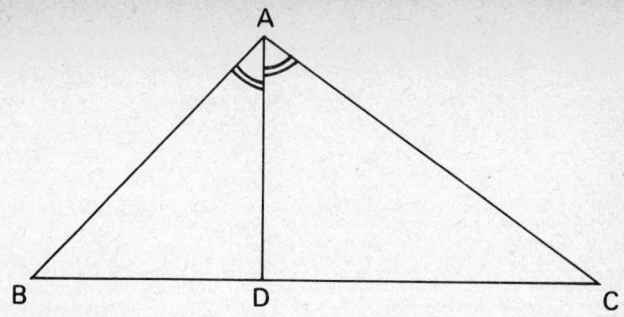

AD bisects ∠ BAC

then $\dfrac{BD}{DC} = \dfrac{AB}{AC}$

Many of the above theorem have important converses. The reader should consider the converse of each theorem and determine whether it is true, and make a note of such results.

EXAMPLES

(A) Numerical

1. ABCDEF is a regular hexagon, AC and BD intersect at X. Find the values of the angles BAC, ACD and AXB. Prove that ACDE is a cyclic quadrilateral.

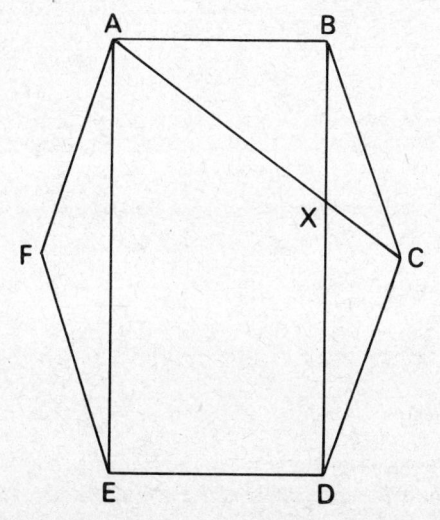

Since ABCDEF is a regular hexagon each exterior angle when the sides are produced in order is $\frac{360°}{6} = 60°$

∴ each interior angle = 120°

OR each interior angle = $\frac{2 \times 6 - 4}{6}$ rt. ∠s = $\frac{8}{6} \times 90° = 120°$

In Δ ABC:
$$AB = BC \text{ (sides regular hexagon)}$$
$$\therefore \angle BAC = \angle BCA \text{ (base ∠s isosceles Δ)}$$
$$\angle ABC = 120° \text{ (∠ of regular hexagon)}$$
$$\therefore \underline{\angle BAC = 30°} \text{ (∠ sum of Δ)}$$
$$\text{also } \angle BCA = 30°$$
$$\angle BCD = 120°$$
$$\therefore \angle ACD = 120° - 30°$$
$$= \underline{90°}$$

Similarly ∠ABD = 90° and ∠AED = 90°

∴ In Δ ABX
$$\angle AXB = 180° - 90° - 30° \text{ (∠ sum of Δ)}$$
$$= \underline{60°}$$

In quad ACDE
$$\angle ACD + \angle AED = 90° + 90°$$
$$= 180°$$
∴ <u>ACDE is a cyclic quadrilateral</u> (opposite angles supp.)

2.

With the data given in the diagram evaluate the size of ∠ PHS.

Calculation

∠ HSP is an exterior angle of △ SWY

$$\therefore \angle HSP = 36° + 57°$$
$$= 93°$$
$$\angle HPS = \angle SYX = 57° \text{ (Exterior } \angle \text{ of cyclic quad. PSXY)}$$
$$\angle PHS = 180° - 93° - 57° \text{ (}\angle \text{ sum of } \triangle\text{)}$$
$$= \underline{30°}$$

3. ATM is a tangent to a circle which touches the circle at T. A secant ABC meets the circle at B and C. The diameter through B meets the circle again at D. If angle DBC = 40° = Angle ATB,
   (a) calculate the values of angle BAT and angle DTM, and
   (b) prove that (i) AC is a parallel to TD, (ii) CT is a diameter.

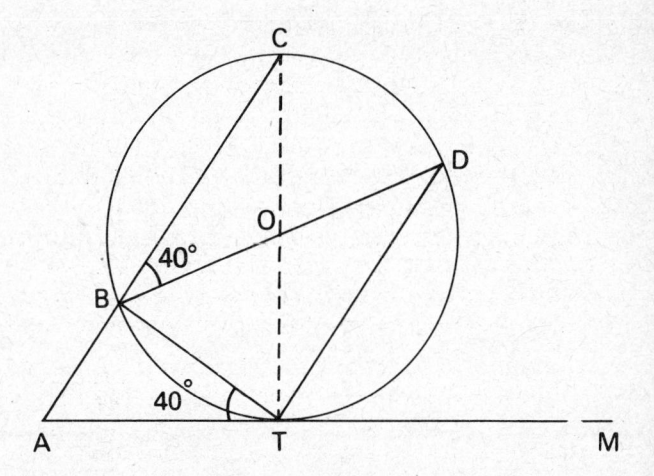

(a) To Find ∠ BAT, ∠ DTM

$$\angle BTD = 90° \text{ (angle in a semi-circle)}$$
$$\angle BDT = \angle ATB \text{ (angle in alternate segment)}$$
$$\therefore \angle BDT = 40°$$
$$\therefore \angle TBD = 50° \text{ (angle sum of } \triangle \text{ BTD)}$$
$$\therefore \angle CBT = 90°$$

But ∠ CBT = ∠ BAT + ∠ BTA (Exterior angle of triangle ABT)

$$\therefore 90° = \angle BAT + 40°$$
$$\therefore \underline{\angle BAT = 50°}$$

$\angle DTM = 180° - \angle BTD - \angle ATB$ (adjacent angles, ATM a str. line)
$$\therefore \angle DTM = 180° - 90° - 40°$$
$$\therefore \underline{\angle DTM = 50°}$$

(b) To Prove (i) AC||TD
    (ii) CT is a diameter

Proof

$\angle BAT = \angle DTM$ (Both 50° from part (a))
$$\therefore \underline{AC||TD} \text{ (corresponding angles equal)}$$

$\angle TBC = \angle TBD + \angle DBC$
$ = 50° + 40$ (found in (a) and given)
$ = 90°$
$$\therefore \underline{CT \text{ is a diameter}}$$

PRACTICE QUESTIONS

1.

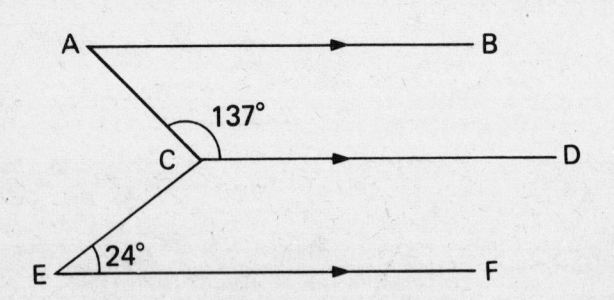

The straight lines AB, CD and EF are parallel.
Find the size of $\angle ACE$.

2. Find the sizes of the angles marked a, b, c and d in the following diagrams.

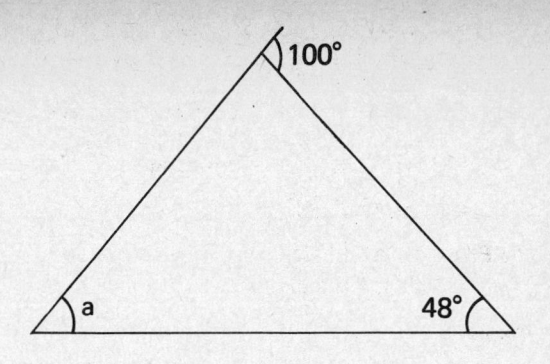

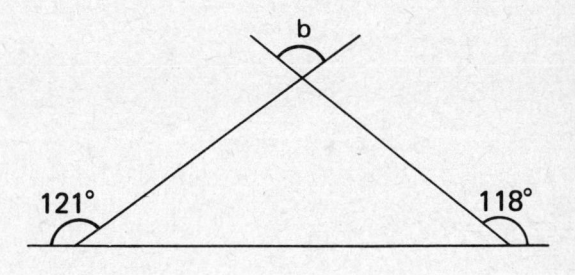

O is the centre of the circle below.

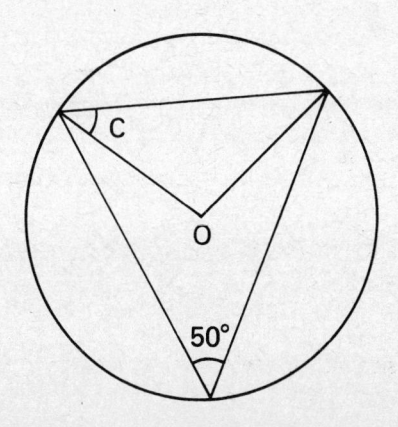

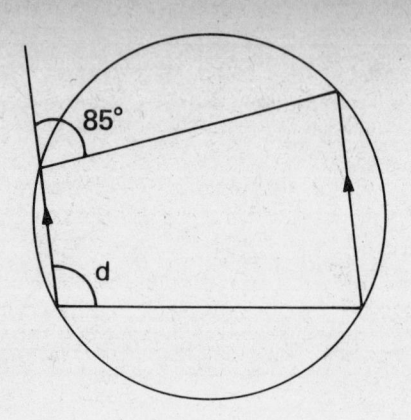

3.

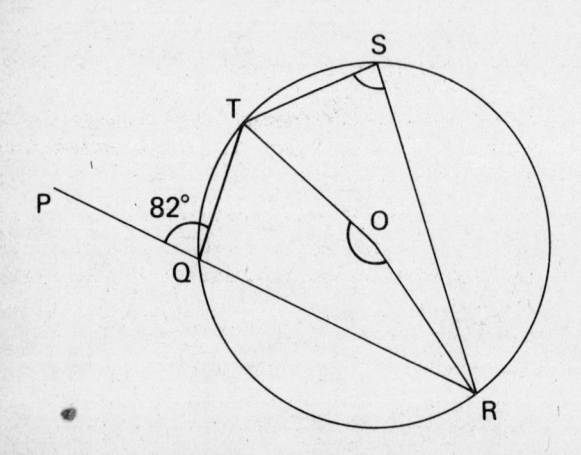

O is the centre of the circle. PQR is a straight line.
Find the values of ∠ TSR and ∠ TOR.

4.

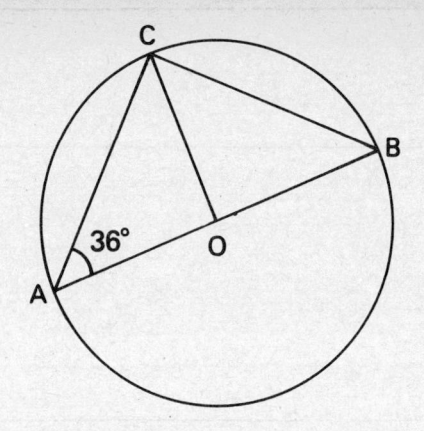

O is the centre of the circle. AB is a diameter and ∠ BAC = 36°.
Calculate the value of   (a) ∠ ABC   (b) ∠ AOC.

5.

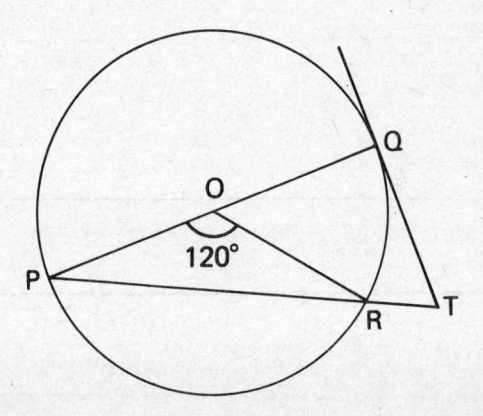

PQ is a diameter of the circle centre O. TQ is a tangent to the circle at Q. ∠ POR is 120°. PRT is a straight line.
Find, giving your reasons, the size of ∠ PTQ.

EXAMPLES

(B) Theoretical

1. Angle C is an obtuse angle in triangle ABC. M is the mid-point of BC. P is a point in AB such that AP = AC. A line parallel to CP is drawn through M meeting AB at R and AC produced at S.
   Prove that RB = CS.

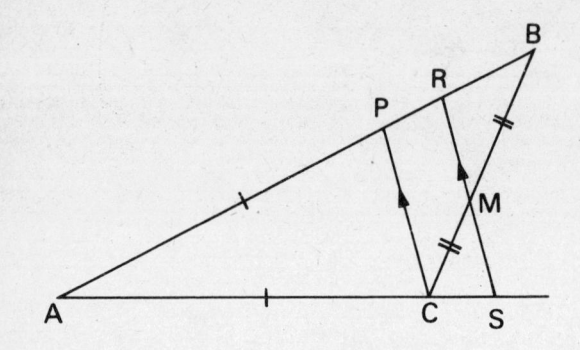

   To Prove RB = CS

   In △ ASR, CP ∥ RS given

   $$\therefore \frac{AP}{PR} = \frac{AC}{CS} \text{ (ratio theorem)}$$

   But AP = AC (given)
   ∴ PR = CS   1

   In △ BPC
   BM = MC and MR ∥ CP (given)
   ∴ BR = PR (intercept theorem)   2

   From 1 and 2
   $\underline{BR = CS}$

2. The diagram shows two concentric circles centre O. PR is a tangent to the smaller circle with point of contact T, AB is a tangent to the smaller circle with point of contact H.
   Prove that AP = BR.

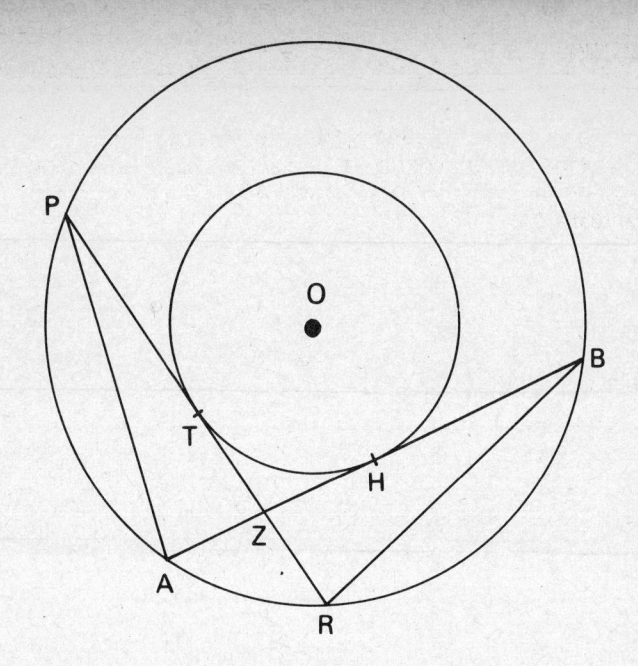

To Prove AP = BR.

Construction Draw OT and OH

Proof ∠ OTP = 90° and ∠ OHB = 90° (tangent perpendicular to radius at point of contact)

OT = OH (radii of smaller circle)

∴ PR and BA are chords equidistant from centre O.

∴ PR = BA

also PT = TR and AH = HB (perpendicular from centre bisects chord)

∴ PT = HB.   **1**

ZT = ZH   **2** (tangents from external point)

Adding **1** and **2**

PZ = BZ.

In Δ APZ and Δ RBZ

(i)   PZ = BZ (Proved)
(ii) ∠ PAZ = ∠ ZRB (Angles in some segment of larger circle)

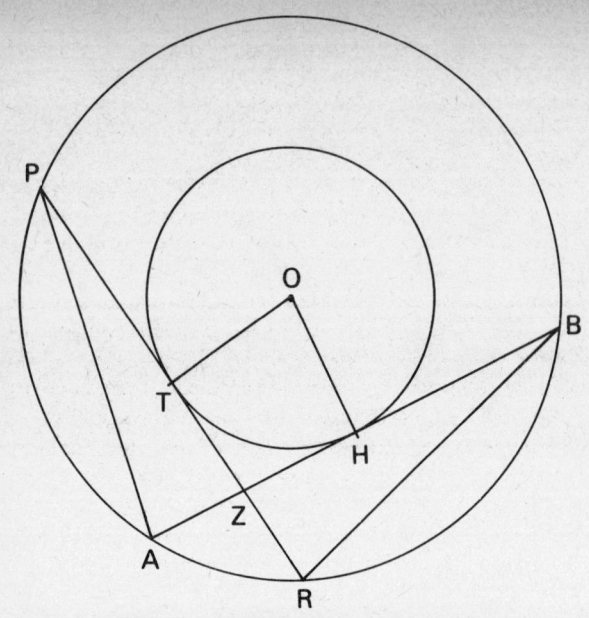

(iii) $\angle$ AZP = $\angle$ RZB (Vertically opposite angles)
∴ $\angle$ APZ ≡ $\triangle$ RBZ (AAS)
∴ AP = BR. (Corresponding sides of congruent triangles)

3. An acute angled triangle ABC is inscribed in a circle so that A, B and C lie on the circle. The altitude of the triangle from A meets BC at P and when produced meets the circle at K. The altitude from B meets AC at M when produced meets the circle at N. The two altitudes intersect at H.

   Prove that:
   (1) A, M, P. B are concyclic.
   (2) $\angle$ KBC = $\angle$ PBM = $\angle$ CAN.
   (3) triangle BHP is congruent to triangle BKP and triangle HMA is congruent to triangle AMN.
   (4) PM is parallel to KN and PM = ½ KN.

   To Prove (1) A, M, P. B are concyclic.
   (2) $\angle$ KBC = $\angle$ PBM = $\angle$ CAN.
   (3) $\triangle$ BHP ≡ $\triangle$ BKP and $\triangle$ HMA ≡ $\triangle$ NMA.
   (4) PM||KN and PM = ½ KN.

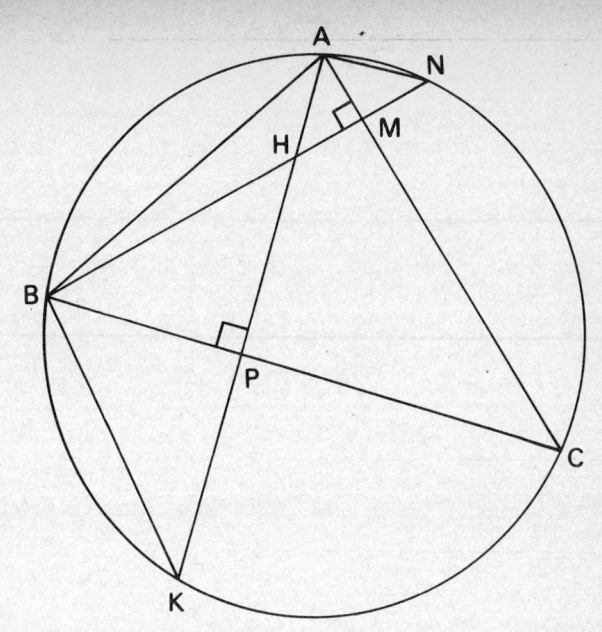

Proof (1)   ∠ BPA = ∠ BMA (both rt. ∠s; altitudes of Δ given)

∴ A, M, P, B are concyclic (AB subtends equal angles on same side).

(2)   ∠ KBC = ∠ KAC (angles in same segment)
∠ KAC = ∠ PAM (same angle)
∠ PAM = ∠ PBM (angles in same segment of circle through A, M, P, B)
∴ ∠ KBC = ∠ PBM
∠ PBM = ∠ CBN (same angle)
∠ CBN = ∠ CAN (angles in same segment)
∴ ∠ PBM = ∠ CAN
∴ ∠ KBC = ∠ PBM = ∠ CAN

(3) In Δs BHP and BKP
 (i)   BP is common
 (ii)   ∠ BPH = ∠ BPK = 90° (AP altitude)
 (iii)   ∠ PBH = ∠ KBP (Proved in (2))
 ∴ Δ BHP ≡ Δ BKP (ASA)

Similarly in Δs HMA and MNA

(i) AM is common
(ii) ∠ HMA = ∠ NMA = 90° (BM altitude)
(iii) ∠ HAM = ∠ NAM (Proved in (2))
∴ <u>Δ HMA ≡ Δ NMA (ASA)</u>

(4) Since Δ BHP ≡ Δ BKP
HP = KP
Since Δ HMA = Δ NMA
HM = NM
∴ In Δ KHN
HP = KP and HM = NM
∴ <u>PM||KN and PM = ½ KN</u> (mid-point theorem)

PRACTICE QUESTIONS

1. ABCD is a parallelogram. The line through D parallel to AC meets BC produced at E. Prove that the triangles ABC, ACD and DCE are congruent.

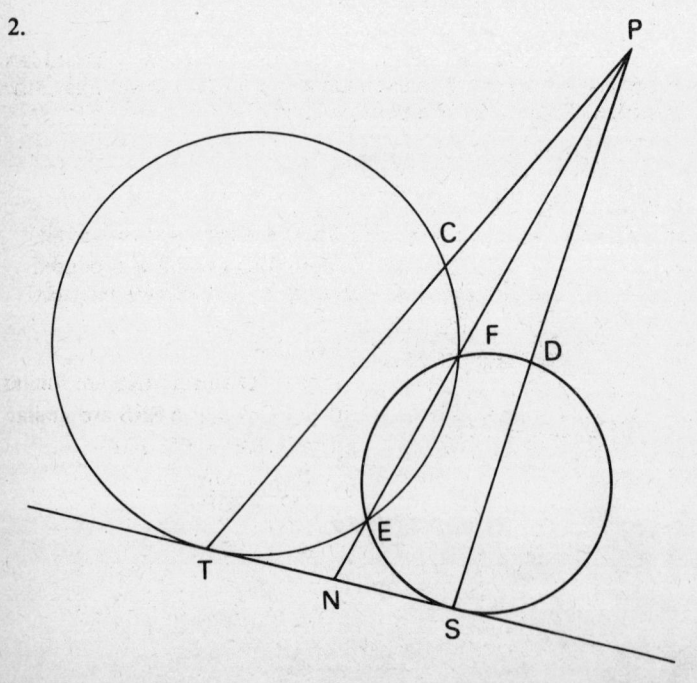

2.

In the diagram T and S are the points of contact of the common tangent TNS to the two circles.

Prove that

(a) PC.CT = PD.PS

(b) TN = NS

3.

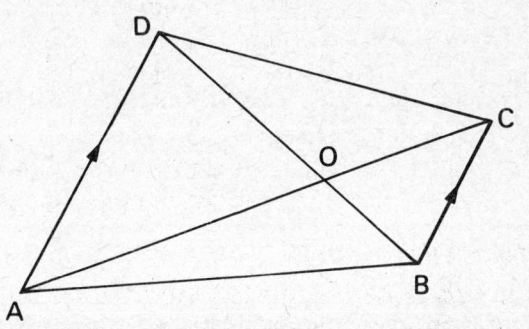

In the figure, AD is parallel to BC. Prove that area triangle DOC = area triangle AOB.

4. P, Q, R and S are the mid-points of the sides AB, BC, CD and DA respectively of the quadrilateral ABCD. Prove that the quadrilateral PQRS is a parallelogram.

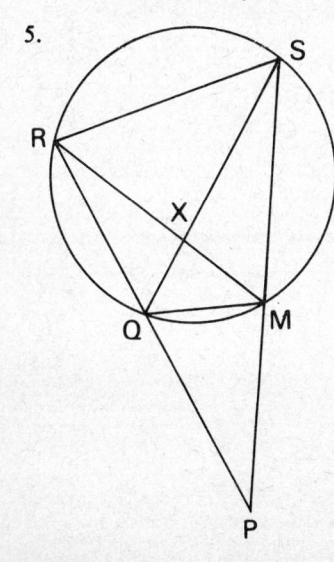

5.

QRSM is a cyclic quadrilateral.

RQ produced and SM produced meet at P. RM and QS intersect at X.

Prove that:

(i) $\triangle$ RXQ and $\triangle$ MXS are similar

(ii) $\triangle$ PQM and $\triangle$ PRS are similar

(iii) PQ, RP = PS, PM

(iv) $\dfrac{MR}{QS} = \dfrac{MP}{QP}$

6. ABCDE is a regular pentagon. BE and AC intersect at X. Calculate ∠ BXC.

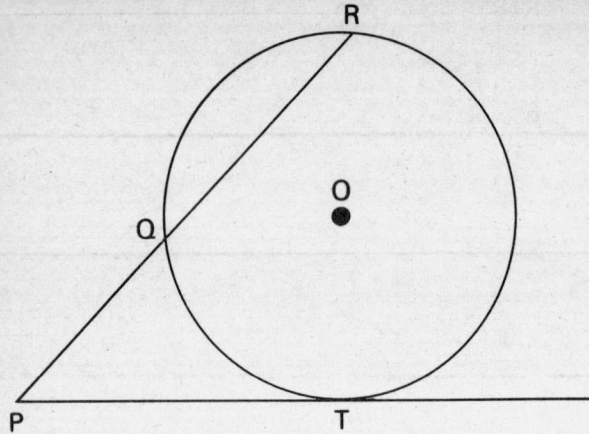

7. In the diagram, PT is a tangent at T to the circle, centre O, radius 10cm. PT = 24cm, PR = 30cm. Calculate:
   (i)   the lengths of OP and QR
   (ii) the ratio QT : TR
   (iii) the size of the angle RPT, correct to the nearest minute
   (iv) the length of the perpendicular from T to PR, correct to 3 s.f.

8. In the diagram, O is the centre of the circle. AC is produced to D. ∠ BCD = 79°. Calculate:
   (i)   ∠ APB,
   (ii) ∠ AOB,
   (iii) ∠ ASC.

9.

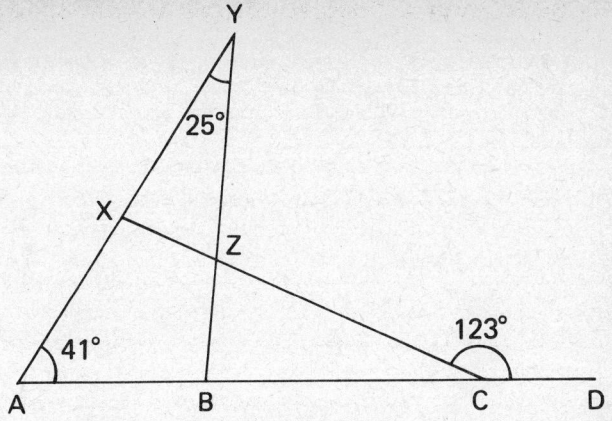

In the diagram ABCD, XZC and YZB are straight lines. Calculate the size of (i) ∠YBC and (ii) ∠XZY.

10.

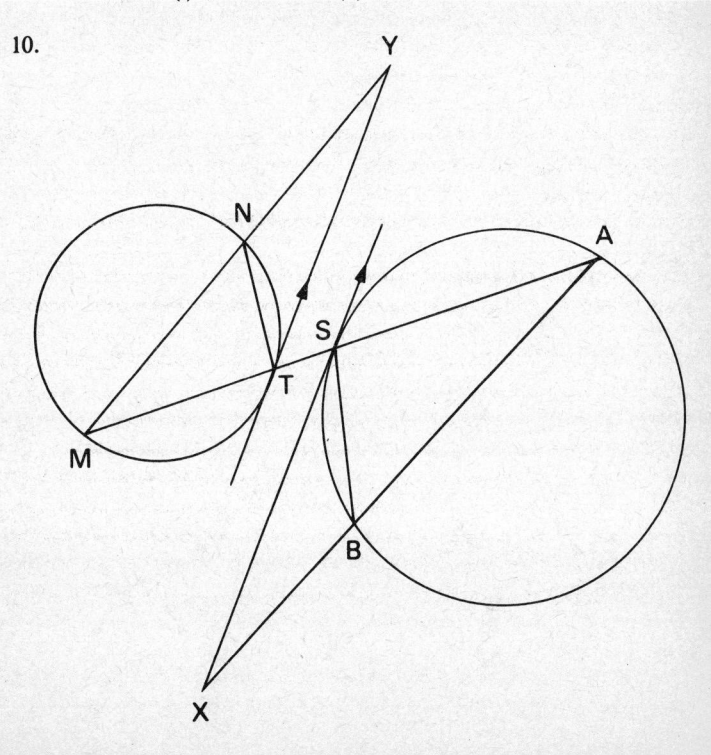

In the diagram MTSA is a straight line which meets the unequal circles at M, T, S and A, such that the tangents at T and S are parallel. The diameters MN, AB produced meet these tangents at Y and X as shown. Prove that

(i) MY||XA

(ii) $\triangle$ ABS is similar to $\triangle$ MNT

(iii) $\triangle$ BXS is similar to $\triangle$ TYN

(iv) $\dfrac{XS}{AB} = \dfrac{TY}{MN}$.

11. In this question ruler and compasses only are to be used.

    Construct triangle ABC with AB = 5cm, BC = 6cm and AC = 7cm. On the opposite side of AC to B, construct triangle ADC with $\angle$ CAD = 90° and $\angle$ ACD = 30°. Through D draw DM parallel to CB, meeting BA produced at M. Measure the length of AM in cms.

EVERYDAY ARITHMETIC

The types of questions set on the payment of gas, electricity and telephone bills, mortgages, H.P., local and national taxes require careful reading by the student before he attempts to answer them. They are then usually straight forward as the following examples show.

EXAMPLES

1. My quarterly electricity bill is made up of a quarterly standing charge of £3.18 in addition to the payment at the rate of 3·857p per unit for the number of units of electricity used.

   What was the total amount of my bill if I had used 962 units of electricity?

   962 units at 3·857p per unit = 3·857 × 962p

                                     = 3710p (fractions of a penny are ignored)

   Total amount owed   = £3.18 + £37.10

                                    = £40.28

2. Five years ago the quarterly rental for my telephone was £7.50 and calls were charged at 1·8p per metered unit. V.A.T. on the total amount was then charged at 8%.

Now the quarterly rental is £8.35, and each metered unit costs 3·3p. V.A.T. is 10%. If my metered units average 400 per quarter what is the percentage increase in the amount I have now to pay compared with 5 years ago?

5 years ago

Cost of metered units	= 1·8p × 400 = 720p.	= £7.20
rental	=	= £7.50
Total payable to Post Office		= £14.70
add V.A.T. at 8%		= £1.17*
Total amount to be paid		= £15.87

*(fractions ignored)

Now

Cost of metered units	= 3·3p × 400 = 1320p	= £13.20
rental		= £8.35
Total payable to Post Office		= £21.55
Add V.A.T. at 10%		= £2.15
		£23.70

Increase in amount I pay = £23.70 − £15.87
= £ 7.83
= $\frac{7 \cdot 83}{15 \cdot 87} \times 100\%$
= 49·34% (to 2 dec. pls.)

3. The cash price of a freeezer is £408. The H.P. charges are a deposit of ⅓ of the cash price and 18 monthly payments of £19.50 each. What is the total H.P. price of the freezer? What annual rate of simple interest is charged on the H.P. debt? (Correct to the nearest whole number.)

H.P. deposit ⅓ of £408	= £136
18 payments of £19.50	= £351
Total H.P. price	= £487
Simple Interest = £487 − £408	= £ 79

$$I = \frac{PRT}{100} \text{ so } R = \frac{100I}{PT}$$

$$R = \frac{100 \times 79}{408 \times 1 \cdot 5} \%$$

rate % S.I.   12·91 = 13% to nearest %

4. A man is paid £1.36 per hour for a basic 37½ hour week. Overtime is paid at the rate of "time and a half" except on Saturday and Sunday when the overtime rate is "double time". Calculate his gross wages when he worked 45 hours including 3 hours on Saturday.

Deductions from his gross earnings are as follows:

Income tax 30% of all earnings over £34 per week.

National Insurance and State Pension 7% of gross weekly earnings.

Union dues 75p per week.

Calculate his "take home" pay. What percentage of his gross pay is deducted (to nearest %)?

Basic pay = £1.86 × 37·5
= £1.86 × 30 + £1.86 × 7 + ½ of £1.86
= £69.75

Total hours overtime worked = 45 − 37½ = 7½.

Overtime at "time and a half" earns 1½ × £1.86 × 4½
= £2.79 × 4·5
= £12.55½.

Overtime at "double time" earns 2 × £1.86 × 3
= £3·72 × 3
= £11.16

<u>Total gross earnings</u> = £69.75 + £12.55½ + £11.16
= <u>£93.46½</u>

Income tax paid = 30% of £59.46½
= £17.83 (fractions of p. ignored)

Nat. Insurance pension = 7% of £93.46½
= £6.54

Total deductions = 75p + £6.54 + £17.83
= £25.12

<u>Take home pay</u> = <u>£68.34½</u>

deductions = $\frac{25 \cdot 12}{93 \cdot 465}$ × 100% of gross

<u>Deductions</u> = <u>27% of gross pay</u>

5. A man on holiday on the Continent spent 200 francs per day on hotels in France and 3220 pesetas per day on hotels in Spain. He spent 4 days in each country. The rates of exchange were

8·66 francs to £1 and 140 pesetas to £1.

Calculate the total amount in pounds, to the nearest ten pence which he spent on hotels during his holiday.

While in France he paid 3 francs per litre for petrol. Find the equivalent cost per gallon in pounds, to nearest penny. Take 1 gal = 4·54 litres.

$$\text{Cost of hotels in France} = 200 \times 4 \text{ francs} = 800 \text{ francs}$$
$$8 \cdot 66 \text{ fr.} = £1$$
$$800 \text{ fr.} = £\frac{800}{8 \cdot 66} = £92.379$$

$$\text{Cost of hotel in Spain} = 3220 \times 4 \text{ pesetas} = 12880 \text{ pesetas}$$
$$140 \text{ pesetas} = £1$$
$$12880 \text{ pesetas} = £\frac{12880}{140} = £92.00$$

<u>Total cost of hotels</u> = £184.379
= <u>£184.40 to nearest 10p.</u>

1 litre of petrol costs 3 fr.
4·54 litres of petrol cost 4·54 × 3 fr.
= 13·62 fr.
8·66 fr. = £1
$13 \cdot 62$ fr. $= £\frac{13 \cdot 62}{8 \cdot 66}$ = £1.573

<u>1 gal. of petrol costs £1.57 to nearest p.</u>

PRACTICE QUESTIONS

1. My quarterly gas bill is made up of a standing charge of £2.50 plus the cost of the therms of gas used. The first 50 therms used are charged at the rate of 23·8p per therm and the remainder at the rate of 16·4p per therm. Calculate my gas bill for the quarter in which I used 397 therms of gas. (Fractions of a penny are ignored in the bill.)

2. The quarterly rental of my telephone is £8.75 and calls are charged at the rate of 3·2p per metered unit. V.A.T. at 10% is added to the total. If I used 687 metered units in a quarter what was the total amount payable?

3. The cash price of a colour T.V. set is £385. The H.P. charges are
   (1) a deposit of ⅓ of the cash price,
   (2) 23 monthly payments of £12.70,
   (3) a final payment of £10.

Calculate the total amount paid under the H.P. scheme.

Regarding the cash price as the principal, the total H.P. price as the amount at the end of 2 years, calculate (to nearest %) the rate of simple interest.

Would the actual rate of interest charged on the H.P. scheme be more or less than the simple interest rate so calculated?

4. A craftsman is paid £2.56 per hour for a 40 hour week. Calculate his gross weekly wage.

    If he receives a $12\frac{1}{2}\%$ increase what will be his new weekly gross wage?

    Deductions from his old gross wage amounted to 25% while deductions from his new gross wage amount to 30%. What is the net increase in his weekly wage? Express this net increase as a percentage of his original net weekly wage.

5. A person changed £200 into Swiss francs at the rate of 3·36 francs to the pound. How many francs were received? The price of petrol in Switzerland was 1·85 francs per litre. Taking 1 gal = 4·54 litres find the cost of petrol in £ per gal, correct to the nearest p.

6. The rateable value of my house is £269. How much do I have to pay when the rate is 97p in the £?

    The rateable value is increased by 10% and the rate in the £ reduced by 5%. How much do I now have to pay (correct to the nearest p.)?

QUICK TEST A

1. (i) Express 1260 in prime factors. By what number must 1260 be multiplied in order that the product is a perfect square?
   (ii) If $y = a(3x - a)$, express x in terms of y and a.
   (iii) One angle of a polygon is 60° and each of the remaining angles is 150°. Find the number of sides of the polygon.

2. Use tables to find the values of the following, correct to 3 significant figures.
   (i) $(47 \cdot 26)^2$ (ii) $(0 \cdot 0871)^2$
   (iii) $\sqrt{(234 \cdot 5)}$ (iv) $\sqrt{(0 \cdot 006728)}$
   (v) $\dfrac{1}{25 \cdot 4}$ (vi) $\dfrac{1}{0 \cdot 4616}$

3. Simplify,
   (i) $\dfrac{x}{2y} + \dfrac{3x}{4y}$ (ii) $\dfrac{8a^3 b}{3c} \times \dfrac{6c^2}{abd}$
   (iii) $\dfrac{3(x-1)}{2} - \dfrac{(2x-5)}{3}$ (iv) $\dfrac{6x}{5ab} \div \dfrac{3x^2}{10a}$

4. In triangle ABC, $\angle ABC = 56°$ and $\angle ACB = 42°$. The bisector of $\angle ABC$ meets AC at P. BP is produced to Q such that AB = AQ. Calculate $\angle BAC$, $\angle QAC$ and $\angle QPC$. What can you deduce about AQ and BC?

5. The individual ages of the members of a pop group are 25, 18, 22, 18, 23 and 20. What is the average (mean) age of the group? The oldest member leaves the group. The age of his replacement is such that the average age of the group is now 20. How old is the newest member of the group?

6. A company's profits rose from £325,000 in one year to £500,000 in the next. Find the percentage increase in the profit. If this percentage increase in profit from one year to the next was expected to be maintained for the next year what will the expected profit be?

7. In triangle ABC, AB = 8cm, BC = 7cm, and CA = 5cm. Show that $\cos A = \frac{1}{2}$. Without using tables write down the value of sin A and the area of the triangle ABC.

8. The circumference of each wheel of a bicycle is 215cm. How many revolutions per minute, correct to 3 significant figures, will each wheel make when the bicycle is travelling at 60km per hour?

9. Find, correct to the nearest penny, the compound interest on £1,260 for 2 years at $9\frac{1}{2}$% per annum.

10. Solve the simultaneous equations
$$3x - 2y = 7$$
$$x + 4y = 7$$

QUICK TEST B

1. (i) Simplify (a) $3x - 4y + 7(4y - 5x)$
   (b) $(5a - 2b)^2 - 3(a^2 - 7b^2)$

   (ii) Factorise (a) $6x^3y - 9x^2y^2$
   (b) $x^2 - 3x - 10$
   (c) $a^2 - 121$

2. Express 16·757   (a) correct to 2 significant figures,
   (b) correct to 2 decimal places,
   (c) in standard form.

   (ii) If $a = 3·75$, $b = 0·0007$, $c = -2·5$ and $d = 0·1$ calculate the values of ad; bd; $2a - c$; d^2; $7a + c^2$; $\dfrac{a}{2d}$.

3. Solve (i) $7x + 9 = 2$
   (ii) $9 + 3(x - 5) = 4 - 7(2 - x)$
   (iii) $\dfrac{x}{6} - \dfrac{x}{8} = \dfrac{5x}{12} + \dfrac{1}{8}$
   (iv) $(x - 3)(x + 2) = (x + 4)(x + 5)$

4.

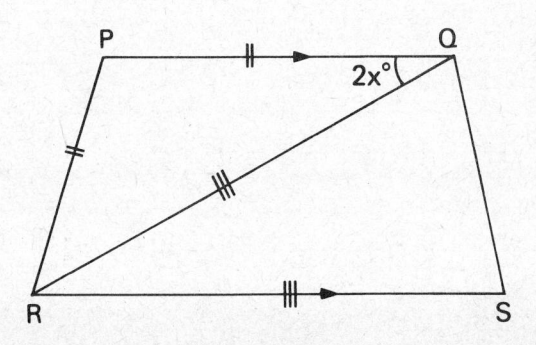

In the diagram PQ is parallel to SR. PQ = PS, SQ = SR. If ∠PQS = $2x°$ express each of the angles PSQ and QSR in terms of x.
If the quadrilateral PQRS is cyclic calculate x.

5. (i) Find the equation of the line passing through the points $(0, -2)$ and $(-3, -8)$
   (ii) If y is proportional to x^2, and if $y = 8$ when $x = 4$, express y in terms of x. Draw a graph to show the connection between y and x for values of x from $x = -6$ to $x = +6$.

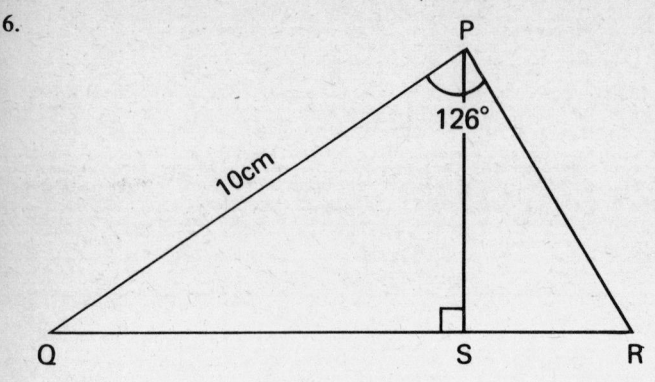

6.

In the diagram, $\angle$ QPR = 126° and $\angle$ PRQ = 2$\angle$ PQR. PS is perpendicular to QR. QP is 10cm.
Calculate (i) QS (ii) PS (iii) SR (iv) Area of triangle PQR.

7. At what rate % per annum will £125 yield a simple interest of £50 in $2\frac{1}{2}$ years?

8. Solve the equation $2x^2 - 9x + 5 = 0$, giving each value of x correct to two decimal places.

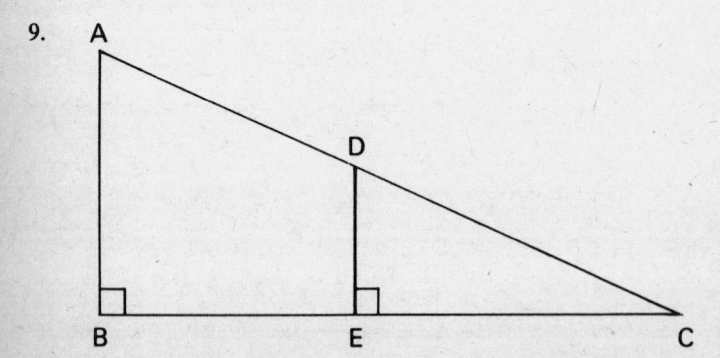

9.

In the diagram, $\angle$ ABC = $\angle$ DEC = 90°. BC = 48cm, AB = 20cm and DE = 5cm. Calculate the lengths of EC and AD.

10. (a) Evaluate (i) $2^2 \times 9^{\frac{1}{2}} \times 3^{-2}$
(ii) $16^{\frac{3}{4}} \div 2^{-1} \div 4^0$
(b) Simplify (i) $\dfrac{2}{x} - \dfrac{4}{x}$
(ii) $\dfrac{2}{x} \div \dfrac{4}{x}$

TEST 1

SECTION A   Attempt all questions

1. Do not use calculators or tables in this question.

   (i) Simplify (a) $3 \cdot 64 \times 200$

                   (b) $0 \cdot 347 \div 0 \cdot 02$

                   (c) $(0 \cdot 5)^3$

                   (d) $\sqrt{0 \cdot 0016}$

   (ii) If $\sin A = \frac{1}{3}$ find $\tan A$.

   (iii) Evaluate $\sqrt{98} \times \sqrt{8} \times \sqrt{27} \times \sqrt{75}$

2. (i) Express algebraically

       (a) the sum of two numbers x and y multiplied by twice a third number z.

       (b) three times a minus b is less than four times the sum of b and c.

   (ii) Simplify (a) $(3x - 4)(7x + 6) - 2(x^2 - 12)$.

                 (b) $3(x^2 - 3x + 4) - 5(z - x - 2x^2)$

                 (c) $(-8x) \times (+4y) \div (-6xy^2)$

3. (i) Solve the equations

       (a) $5(x - 3) = 7 - (x - 5)$

       (b) $\dfrac{3x}{2} - \dfrac{4 - x}{3} = \dfrac{1}{2}$

   (ii) Solve the simultaneous equations

   $$a - 3b = 2$$
   $$10a - 12b = 17$$

4. A teenager is paid £1.86 per hour for a basic 38 hour week. Overtime is paid at the rate of "time and a half" on Monday to Friday and "double time" for Saturday and Sunday. Calculate his gross wage in a week when he worked 47 hours including 2 hours a day on Saturday and Sunday. Deductions from his gross pay were calculated as follows:

   (i) Income tax 25% of gross pay.

   (ii) National Insurance 5% of gross pay.

   Calculate his net pay.

SECTION B

Attempt any 3 questions

5. A flat car park of area 2134m² is flooded to a depth of 25cm. Calculate correct, to 3 significant figures, the weight of water on the car park in tonnes. How long will it take for the car park to be clear of water if water is drained into 4 drains each of cross-section 1m², and water flows in each drain at an average speed of 2·5m per hour.

6. An isosceles triangle ABC is inscribed in a circle. $\angle$ ABC = $\angle$ ACB = 2 $\angle$ BAC. The bisector of angle ABC meets the circle at D and the bisector of angle ACB meets the circle at E. Prove that ADCBE is a regular pentagon.

7. A cyclist leaves home at noon to travel to a town 10km away cycling at a steady speed of 12km/hour. $12\frac{1}{2}$ minutes later he had a puncture which he repaired in 10 minutes and then continued on his journey at a steady speed of 30km/hour. Draw an accurate distance-time graph of his journey with a scale of 2cm for 5 mins on the time axis and a scale of 2cm for 1km on the distance axis. From your graph determine the time of the cyclist's arrival at the town.

A second cyclist left the town at noon travelling at a steady speed of 15km/hour along the road towards the first cyclist's home.

By drawing appropriate lines on your graph determine where and when they met and also at what times were they 1km apart.

8.

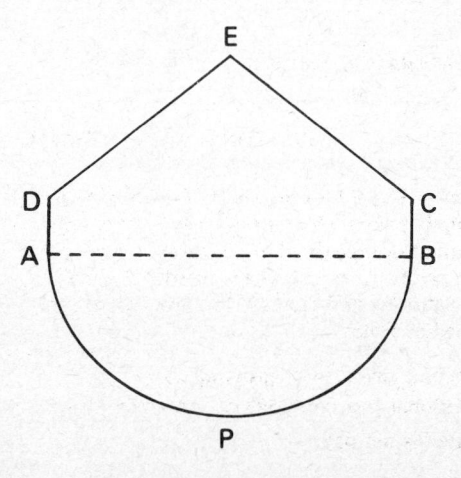

The diagram shows the cross-section of a toy consisting of a solid rubber base APB in the shape of a hemisphere of radius 10cm and a hollow plastic top in two parts. ABCD is a hollow cylinder of height 4cm surmounted by a hollow cone DEC. The total height of the toy is 30cm. Calculate:

(a) the volume of rubber used in the base;

(b) the total area of plastic used;

(c) the total mass of the toy if the density of the rubber is 2·6g per cm^3 and the plastic weighs 0·7g per cm^2.

9. Use ruler and compasses only in this construction.

(i) Draw a line AB 7cm in length. Construct the positions of the points which are equidistant from A and B and also 6cm from A.

(ii) Construct quadrilateral ABCD in which AB = 8·2cm, AC = 9cm, ∠ BAC = 60°, AD = DC and ∠ ADC = 90°.

TEST 2

Answer all questions from section A and three from section B

SECTION A

1. (i) Simplify (a) $\dfrac{3a^2b}{4xy^3} \div \dfrac{6a^3b^2}{xy}$ (b) $\dfrac{5}{6} - \dfrac{x-3}{3}$

   (ii) Calculate the difference between the simple and compound interest on a Principal of £1,000 invested for 2 years at a rate of 12% per annum.

2. (i) Find x when $3(x - a) = bx + 3$

   (ii) Solve the simultaneous equations
   $$y = x - 7$$
   $$x^2 - y^2 - 77$$

3. Triangle ABC is right angled at B. $\angle ACB = 30°$, CB = 15cm, BA is produced to D such that $\angle ADC = 55°$. M. is the mid-point of AD. Calculate:

   (a) AB (b) AD (c) $\angle CMB$.

4. (i) Find the equation of the line joining A(-3, 4) to B(7, -6).

   (ii) Write down the values of sin 137° 52' and tan 152° 37'.

   (iii) The cash price of a freezer is £300. To buy the freezer on H.P. costs a deposit of £84 and 24 monthly payments of £14. What is the total H.P. price of the freezer? Taking the H.P. charge as equivalent to the simple interest on £300 for 2 years what is the rate per cent per annum?

SECTION B

5. (i) Prove that $x - 5$ is a factor of $6x^3 - 35x^2 + 19x + 30$ and hence solve the equation $6x^3 - 35x^2 + 19x + 30 = 0$.

   (ii) The length of the hypotenuse of a right angled triangle is $2(3x - 1)$cm. The lengths of the other two sides are 4xcm and $(4x + 2)$cm. Find the value of x.

6. A ball is projected vertically upward from ground level. After t secs. the height h metres of the ball above ground level is given by:
$$h = 30t - 4 \cdot 9t^2.$$

Complete the following table of values of h for given values of t.

t =	0	1	2	3	4	5	6	7
h =	0	25·1	40·4	45·9	41·6			

Using 2cm to represent 1 sec. on the t axis and 2cm to represent 10m on the h axis, draw a graph to show the variation of h with t as t varies from 0 to 7 secs.

From your graph, or otherwise, obtain:

(i) the greatest height reached by the ball;
(ii) the time when the ball was again at ground level;
(iii) the time for which the ball was 30m or more above the ground;
(iv) the speed of the ball when t = 1·5 and when t = 5.

Give a meaning to your value of h when t = 7.

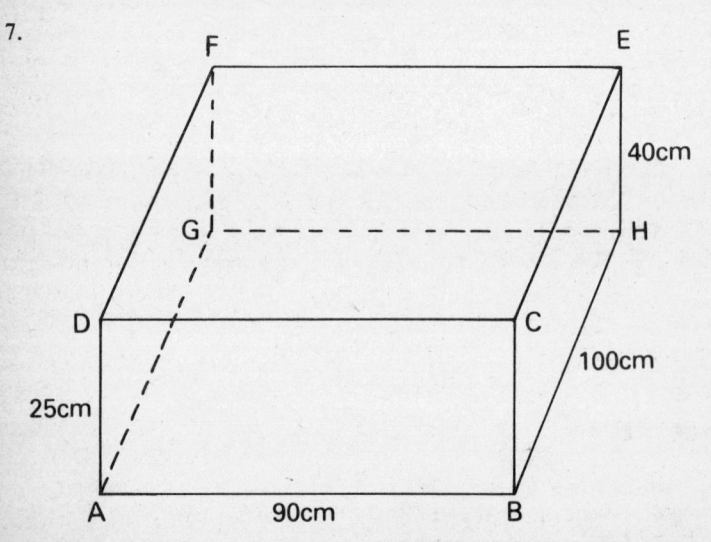

7.

The figure shows a desk with a sloping lid DCEF. The desk is 25cm deep at the front and 40cm deep at the back. The horizontal base is a rectangle 90cm by 100cm as shown. Calculate:

(i) the dimensions of the lid of the desk (FECD);
(ii) the angle that the lid makes with the horizontal;
(iii) the angle that the diagonal DE makes with the horizontal;
(iv) the volume of the desk.

8. PQRS is a straight line such that PQ = RS = ½QR. QRUZ is a square. UP and ZS meet at E. EF is parallel to PS meeting ZP at F. EM and FN are perpendiculars from E and F to PQ meeting PQ at M and N. Prove that NMEF is a square.

9. (a) A and B are two coplanar points 8cm apart. State the locus of a point P moving in the plane such that
   (i) AP = BP (ii) ∠APB = 90°.

   (b) Use ruler and compasses only to construct a rhombus ABCD with sides of length 8cm and ∠BAD = 30°. Draw a circle centre A radius 4cm. Construct the tangents from C to this circle.

ANSWERS TO NUMERICAL QUESTIONS

PAGE 2

1. (i) $2^2 \times 3 \times 13$ (ii) 1, 2, 3, 4, 6, 12, 18, 36, 54, 108
   (iii) $2^2 \times 3^2$, $2 \times 3^2 \times 7$ 18   252

2. $2^2 \times 3^4 \times 5^2 \times 11^2$ $2 \times 3^2 \times 5 \times 11$

3. 462

4. 43

5. 520m   8 poles

6. $3^4 \times 2^4 \times 7^2$ 252

7. $2^6 \times 3^3 \times 5^3$ 60

8. 266   2·5cm

9. 3675m   105m

PAGE 4

1. (i) $7\frac{17}{24}$ (ii) $8\frac{23}{24}$ (iii) 4 (iv) $5\frac{1}{2}$

2. (i) $\frac{7x}{12}$ (ii) $\frac{9-b}{3ab}$

3. (i) $2\frac{2}{6}$ (ii) $6\frac{1}{4}$ (iii) $3\frac{1}{2}$ (iv) $3\frac{3}{24}$

4. (i) $\frac{1}{6}$ (ii) $\frac{7}{8}$

5. $2\frac{31}{48}$

6. (i) 2 (ii) $\frac{15bp}{2a}$

7. (i) $\frac{14x-5}{6}$ (ii) $\frac{x}{5}$

8. (i) $\frac{2y}{3x^4}$ (ii) $\frac{47}{3a}$

9. (i) $6\frac{1}{4}$km (ii) $41\frac{1}{4}$km (iii) $\frac{11x}{24}$ km

10. (i) $\frac{4x^2 + 7x + 15}{5(x-2)}$ (ii) $3\frac{1}{4}$

11. (i) $\frac{7}{30}$ (ii) $\frac{2}{3(x-3)}$

115

PAGE 6

1. 42·339
2. 84·36
3. 54·7938
4. 2·35
5. 567
6. 25·8
7. (i) $1·1 \times 10^{-6}$
   (ii) $5·398 \times 10^4$
8. $1·1332182 \times 10^1$

PAGE 7

1. (i) 162   (ii) 2:3   (iii) £3000 £3500
2. £3000
3. (a) 1:160000   (b) 11·84km   (c) 6·7cm
   (d) 8·96km^2
4. (a) 16200   (b) 125000
5. 7·5cm   6·75cm
6. (i) 6:1   (ii) 27:20   100:(100 − x)
7. 700

PAGE 9

1. $66\frac{1}{3}$%   73% $262\frac{1}{2}$%   80%   36·8%
2. $\frac{9}{20}$ $\frac{1}{8}$ $\frac{3}{40}$
3. (i) £2.25   (ii) £10
4. (i) £78.40   (ii) 38 hrs 48 mins
5. £7.28
6. £1800   £432
7. £1588
8. £2917
9. 18·75%
10. 80%
11. 9p
12. 25%
13. £217.36   4·5%

PAGE 12

1. £204
2. £3200
3. £262.50
4. £20.78
5. £5618
6. £576.19

PAGE 13

1. 8 4 $\frac{1}{125}$ 8 $\frac{1}{121}$ 2. a^{10} a^2 x^2 x^8 b^5 c^{12}
3. $\frac{1}{2}$ 25 1 4 5 1000 $\frac{1}{2}$ 4
4. (i) $28a^2$ (ii) $-4x^2$
5. (i) a^2 (ii) b^4 (iii) x^{13} (iv) $3y^2$

PAGE 16

1. (i) 26470   (ii) 0·318   (iii) 8·807
   (iv) 6739   (v) 1·143
   (vi) 2000000000 = 2×10^9
   (vii) 9·41   (viii) 0·501
2. (i) 98·63   (ii) 627·3   (iii) 0·252   (iv) 0·234

PAGE 17

1. (i) 4120   (ii) 0·119   (iii) 618000   (iv) $9·44 \times 10^{-3}$
2. (i) 9·40   (ii) 0·672   (iii) 25·6
   (iv) 88·8   (v) 0·0686   (vi) 0·027
3. (i) 2·13   (ii) 1·56   (iii) 0·71   (iv) 6·93

PAGE 18

1. (i) 0·138   (ii) 22·1   (iii) $3·48 \times 10^{-3}$
   (iv) 1·82   (v) $5·95 \times 10^{-3}$ (vi) 128·8
   (vii) $1·84 \times 10^{-6}$ (viii) $4·96 \times 10^{-3}$ (ix) $1·08 \times 10^4$
   (x) $1·11 \times 10^{-5}$

PAGE 19

1. 21·7g
2. 240·614m
3. 286mm
4. $\frac{xb + yq}{b + g}$ years
5. 14 years 4 months
6. 110km/hr
7. $32\frac{1}{2}$km/hr
8. £700, £2025
9. 123, 90km.hr^{-1}

PAGE 22

1. $3x(2 - x)$ $(b - 2)(b - 5)$ $(2x + 1)(x + 2)$ $(x + 9)(x - 9)$
   $(12 + b)(12 - b)$ $3cd(5d + 6c)$ $(c + d)(x + y)$ $(a - b)(4 - x)$
   $(3 - y)(9 + 3y + y^2)$ $2(a^2 + b^2)$

2. (i) $x^2a^2(5z + 6x)$ (ii) $(3a + b)(3a - b)$
   (iii) $2(2a + 7)^2$ (iv) $2a(a^2 + 4b^2)$
   (v) $(x - 12y)(x - 2y)$ (vi) $(pq - 1)(r + 2)$
3. (i) $(12x + 5y^3)(12x - 5y^3)$ (ii) no factors
   (iii) $(x + 4y)(x^2 - 4xy + 16y^2)$ (iv) $(x - 4y)(x^2 + 4xy + 16y^2)$

PAGE 23

1. (i) $(x - 2)(x - 3)$
   (ii) (a) 38   (b) 8   (c) $6\frac{10}{27}$
2. $(x - 3)(x + 2)$ 3. -2
4. $(x - 2)(x + 3)(x - 4)$
5. (i) $(x + 2)(x^2 - 2x + 4)$ (ii) $(5y - b)(25y^2 + 5yb + b^2)$
   (iii) $2(6a - b^2)(36a^2 + 6ab^2 + b^4)$
6. $a = 3$ $b = 4$ $(x + 2)$
7. (i) $(x - 2)(x + 2)(x - 3)(x + 3)$
   (ii) $(x - y)(x + y)(x^2 + xy + y^2)(x^2 - xy + y^2)\frac{1}{2}$
8. $c = -2$ $d = 120$ $(x + 2)(x - 3)(x - 5)(x + 4)$

PAGE 28

1. (a) $50 \cdot 4 m^3$ (b) 4460g
2. (a) $270°$ (b) $35 \cdot 3$cm   (c) 133cm^2
3. (a) 1060cm^2 (b) 2280cm^3
4. 8880mm^2
5. 587kg   6. $41 \cdot 7$cm
7. $27 \cdot 52$cm   8. 7081cm^3
9. (a) 12cm   (b) 400cm^3 (c) ⅝ $67°23'$ (d) 360cm^2
10. $5 \cdot 16$cm^3 £38.73
11. 23cm^2 $6\frac{2}{3}$cm

PAGE 32

1. 3   6   4   24
2. 6 $2\frac{1}{2}$ 11   6
3. 2
4. (i) $-4\frac{1}{2}$ (ii) $-\frac{1}{2}$
5. (i) $\frac{1}{2}$ (ii) $\dfrac{14p}{2b - 3}$

6. (i) $1\frac{1}{2}$ (ii) $\dfrac{3c^2}{3ac - 2}$

7. $1\frac{1}{2}$

8. (i) -1 (ii) 2

9. 7

10. $\dfrac{b - a}{3}$ $a - 3b - 4$ $\dfrac{b - 2}{3 - a}$ $\pm 2b - a$

PAGE 35

1. 18   2. 1 hour 55 min
3. 5km   4. 5
5. 8.40 a.m.   2km from home

PAGE 38

1. (i) ± 14 (ii) -20 14   (iii) 2 6   (iv) $-\frac{2}{3}$ 3
2. (i) -2 $\frac{1}{2}$ (ii) $-\frac{1}{3}$ 1   (iii) -3 2
3. (i) $-1\cdot 27$ $2\cdot 77$ (ii) $-9\cdot 10$ $1\cdot 10$
4. (i) $-\frac{1}{2}$ $\frac{1}{6}$ (ii) $-0\cdot 57$ $0\cdot 44$ (iii) $-1\frac{1}{4}$ 2
  (iv) $-\frac{7}{8}$ 1   (v) $1\cdot 27$ $3\cdot 06$

PAGE 39

1. 45 years   2. 14m
3. -7 or 12   4. 11 13
5. 48km per hour

PAGE 42

1. (4, 3)   2. $(-4, 6)$ 3. $(\frac{1}{2}, 2\frac{1}{2})$
4. $(2, -3)$ 5. $(-\frac{1}{4}, -\frac{1}{2})$ 6. (6, 10)
7. $(-3, -5)$

PAGE 43

1. $(-3, 1)$ or $(-\frac{1}{5}, -\frac{3}{5})$ 2. $(3, -2)$ or $(-2\frac{1}{5}, 3\frac{1}{5})$
3. $(4, -1)$ or $(1\frac{1}{2}, 2\frac{1}{2})$ 4. $(-2, \frac{1}{2})$ or $(\frac{1}{3}, \frac{11}{12})$

PAGE 44

1. 36   2. 8 (10p) 11 (50p)
3. £2.50 60p   4. $\frac{4}{7}$
5. 42 7 years

PAGE 47

1. 5
2. $2x + 3y - 13 = 0$
3. (8, 6)　$2y = x + 4$　(0, 2)

PAGE 49

1. 350km　8.30 p.m.
2. 60km/hr　1.20 p.m. to 2.p.m.
   24km/hr　30km/hr
3. 11　11·40　60　120

PAGE 53

1. $-1·7$　$4·7$　$0·5$

PAGE 56

1. (a) 25·5
   (b) 5
   (c) $y = 5x - 38$
   (d) $y = 5x + 1$

2.
$x =$	$-\frac{1}{2}$	0	$\frac{1}{2}$	1	2	$2\frac{1}{2}$	3	$3\frac{1}{2}$	5
$x^2 - 4x + 2 =$	$5\frac{1}{4}$	2	$\frac{1}{4}$	-1	-2	$-1\frac{1}{4}$	-1	$\frac{1}{4}$	7

   (a) 0·58, 3·42
   (b) $-0·24, 4·24$
   (c) $-0·45 < x < 4·45$
   (d) $x \leqslant -0·65$ and $\geqslant 4·65$
   (e) -2

3.
$x =$	1	3	4	6	7	8
$y =$	13	7	7	8	8·71	9·5

   Minimum 6·93　　$x = 1·46$　6·75

4. 7·2 hours　3·5 hours

5. 0·22　3·2

PAGE 62

1.
	sine	cosine	tangent
(a)	0·5777	0·8163	0·7077
(b)	0·7711	$-0·6367$	$-1·2109$
(c)	$-0·3073$	$-0·9516$	0·3230
(d)	$-0·6428$	0·7660	$-0·8391$

2. (i) $\bar{1}·5960$　　(ii) 0·3785
   (iii) $\bar{1}·8314$　　(iv) $\bar{1}·9951$

3. (i) 3·866　　(ii) 6
   (iii) $-0·8391$　　(iv) 0·8473

PAGE 65

1. 9·23cm 11·8cm 14·6cm
2. 13·8cm 12·0cm 16·8cm 112cm^2
3. 6·74cm 13·0cm 87·3cm^2
4. 7·59km 9·57km

PAGE 68

1. 6·65km
2. 17·9cm 116° 2′
3. 11·37km hr^{-1} 208° 24′
4. BC = 32·30mm $\angle$ BCA = 111° 44′ BD = 30mm CD = 12·0mm
5. (a) 53° 20′   (b) 11·7cm   (c) 243cm^2

PAGE 71

1. $3\frac{1}{2}$ − 5 $7\frac{1}{2}$
2. $-\frac{2}{3}$ 6
3. 4 secs
4. 1·5m
5. (a) 8 times (b) $2^{-\frac{1}{3}}$s
6. 40 −3
7. 8cm by 8cm

PAGE 86

1. 67°
2. 52° 59° 40° 95°
3. 82° 164°
4. 54° 108°
5. 60°

PAGE 94

6. 72°
7. (i) 26cm 10·8cm
   (ii) 4:5
   (iii) 41° 30′
   (iv) 15·9cm
8. 79° 158° 101°
9. 66° 57°
11. 2·9cm

PAGE 101

1. £71.30
2. £33.80
3. £456.10 9%
4. £102.40 £115.20
   £3.84 5%
5. 672fr. £2.50
6. £260.93 £272.67

121

QUICK TEST A

1. (i) 2^2 3^2 5 7 35   (ii) $x = \frac{1}{2}(a + \frac{y}{a})$
   (iii) 9
2. (i) 2230   (ii) $7 \cdot 59 \times 10^{-3}$ or $0 \cdot 00759$
   (iii) $15 \cdot 3$ (iv) $0 \cdot 0820$
   (v) $0 \cdot 0394$ (vi) $2 \cdot 17$
3. (i) $\frac{5x}{4y}$ (ii) $\frac{16a^2 3}{d}$ (iii) $\frac{5x + 11}{6}$ (iv) $\frac{4}{bx}$
4. 82° 42° 70° parallel
5. 21 years 19 years
6. 35% £675,000
7. $\frac{\sqrt{3}}{2}$ $10\sqrt{3}$cm^2
8. $46 \cdot 5$
9. £250·77
10. $x = 3, y = 1$

QUICK TEST B

1. (i) $24y - 32x$ $22a^2 - 20ab + 25b^2$
   (ii) $3x^2y(2x - 3y)$ $(x - 5)(x + 2)$ $(a + 11)(a - 11)$
2. (i) 17 $16 \cdot 76$ $1 \cdot 6757 \times 10^1$
   (ii) $0 \cdot 375$ $0 \cdot 00007$ 10 $0 \cdot 01$ $32 \cdot 5$ $18 \cdot 75$
3. (i) -1 (ii) 1   (iii) $-\frac{1}{2}$ (iv) $-1 \cdot 4$
4. $2x°$ $2x°$ $18°$
5. (i) $y = 2x - 2$ (ii) $y = \frac{1}{2}x^2$
6. (i) $9 \cdot 511$cm   (ii) $3 \cdot 090$cm   (iii) $4 \cdot 253$cm   (iv) $21 \cdot 27$cm^2
7. 16%
8. $8 \cdot 85$ $0 \cdot 65$
9. 12cm 39cm
10. $\frac{1}{2}$ 16

TEST 1—PAGE 108

1. (i) 728 $17 \cdot 35$ $0 \cdot 125$ $0 \cdot 04$
   (ii) $\frac{1}{2}$
   (iii) 1260
2. (i) $2z(x + y)$ $(3a - b) < 4(b + c)$

(ii) $19x^2 - 10x$ $13x^2 - 4x + 2$ $\dfrac{16}{3y}$

3. (i) $4\tfrac{1}{2}$ $1\tfrac{4}{5}$ (ii) $a = 1\tfrac{1}{2}$ $b = -\tfrac{1}{8}$
4. £99.51 £66.34
5. 533·5 tonnes 53 hrs. 21 mins.
7. $12\cdot37\tfrac{1}{2}$ $12\cdot25$ $12\cdot23\tfrac{1}{2}$ $12\cdot26\tfrac{1}{2}$
8. 2094cm³ 844·1cm² 6035g

TEST 2—PAGE 111

1. (i) $\dfrac{1}{8aby^2}$ $\dfrac{11 - 2x}{6}$ (ii) £14.40

2. (i) $\dfrac{3 + 3a}{3 - b}$ (ii) $x - 9, y = 2$
3. (a) 8·66cm (b) 1·86cm (c) 57° 25′
4. (i) $x + y = 1$ (ii) $0\cdot6709$ $-0\cdot5180$ (iii) £420 20%
5. (i) 5 $1\tfrac{1}{2}$ $-\tfrac{2}{3}$ (ii) 10
6. (i) 45·9m (ii) 6·1 sec
   (iii) between 1·3 sec and 4·9 sec (iv) $15\cdot3\text{ms}^{-1}$ 19ms^{-1}
7. (i) 101·1cm by 90cm (ii) 8° 32′
   (iii) 6° 22′ (iv) 292500cm³

EXAMINATION TECHNIQUE

Examination revision is a personal thing and you will have evolved your own method of working but you should never forget the reason why you are revising. You are revising to prepare yourself to take (and pass) an examination in this particular subject.

There are various points about taking examinations which you should always remember, some of these may seem obvious but it is amazing how many times they are forgotten.

1. Make sure that you know on which day, at what time and where your examination is to take place.

2. Read through your notes the night before but get enough sleep and do not stay up too late. On the day, arrive in the examination room on time.

3. Make sure that you have brought with you everything you may need (pens, ink, pencils, etc).

4. Read the question paper carefully. Read every question thoroughly before you start to answer any questions.

5. Read the rubrics. If there is a compulsory section, it is wisest to do this first.

6. Plan your time carefully. Work out how much time you should allow for each question and remember to leave some time for reading through what you have written before the end of the examination.

7. After the compulsory question has been answered (if any), answer what you consider to be the easiest question. You should then proceed to the more difficult ones.

8. Write in clear, straight forward English. Do not use abbreviations except in actual words spoken and avoid slang, clichés and colloquial writing.

9. Make sure that you understand what the examiner wants before you answer the question. If you are not sure, try another question. One of the main causes of failure is not answering the actual question which has been set.

10. Diagrams, maps and sketches are often essential. These should add to your written work and if clear, useful and relevant should gain you extra marks. If you are given a diagram or map on the question paper, you can gain no extra marks by copying it.

11. Write legibly and avoid crossing out. If you must cross out work because you feel that you can do better on another question one straight line through the work you do not want marked is enough.

NOTES

NOTES

NOTES

NOTES

NOTES

REVISION MADE EASY!

Now Celtic Revision Aids provide you with the complete programme for revision for O-level and other 16+ examinations.

For each mainstream subject there is a compact two book series:

Rapid Revision Notes O-level is the volume which covers your subject syllabus, explaining clearly and concisely what you need to know for the exam. This book is designed to be used alongside your own course notes for long-term revision, or to be dipped into nearer the exam to remind you of your facts.

Rapid Revision Notes-Examination Practice are just that, practice in all the types of exam question that you will come up against on the day. Essays, multiple choice, data response are all explained, you are told what the examiner expects to see and how to achieve the best possible answer. Each question type is demonstrated with suggested answers and at the back there are lists of questions of all types for you to practice answering.

The sort of simple line drawings or graphs which you can easily understand and reproduce are included where appropriate, in both series.

Series and titles available:

Rapid Revision Notes O-level

Titles: English Language, Mathematics, Physics, Chemistry, Biology, Human Biology, Computer Studies, Commerce, Economics, Sociology, British Economic History, Integrated Science, Commercial Mathematics, Accounts

Rapid Revision Examination Practice O-level

Titles: English Language, Mathematics, Physics, Chemistry, Biology, Human Biology, Computer Studies, Commerce, Economics, Sociology, British Economic History, Integrated Science, Commercial Mathematics, Accounts

Rapid Revision Notes A-level

Titles: Pure Mathematics, Applied Mathematics, Statistics, Biology, Botany, Zoology, Inorganic Chemistry, Organic Chemistry, Physical Chemistry, Physics – Mechanics, Physics – Heat, Light and Sound, Physics – Electricity and Magnetism

Literature Revision Notes & Examples

New Testament Studies O-level

Celtic Revision Notes Law

If you experience difficulty in obtaining a Celtic Revision Aids' title you can order it by writing to:

Sphere Books
Cash Sales Department
PO Box 11
Falmouth
Cornwall   TR10 9EN

Please enclose a cheque or postal order to the value of the cover price plus:
UK: 45p for the first book, 20p for the second book and 14p for each additional book ordered to a maximum charge of £1.63.
OVERSEAS: 75p for the first book plus 21p per copy for each additional book.
BFPL and Eire: 45p for the first book, 20p for the second book plus 14p per copy for the next seven books, thereafter 8p per book.

Sphere Books reserve the right to show new retail prices on covers which may differ from those previously advertised in the text or elsewhere, and to increase postal rates in accordance with the Post Office.

Any general enquiries about Celtic series' should be addressed to:
Celtic Revision Aids Enquiries Department
30–32 Gray's Inn Road
London   WC1